Praise for

FEARLESS CAPTIVATING UNSTOPPABLE

"Cobey is among the foremost public speaking coaches and teachers working in the country. In this book, he deftly pairs the messaging smarts refined in those experiences with the training that makes him a terrific actor. In doing so, he shares his indispensable insight in witty and effortless prose. Best of all, he provides clear, actionable tasks, instilling his readers with the confidence to carry these tasks out. *Fearless Captivating Unstoppable* is a vital read that will make you the strongest, most confident version of you."

— Scott Ellis, Emmy nominated television director of *30 Rock*

"Mandarino's tightly written primer on the foundational elements for becoming a powerful speaker should be owned, dogeared, and taken to heart by both the confident professional and the novice full of terror. His guide is a *tour de force* of practical wisdom showing how one overcomes that fear, but it is more than that. With his engaging and witty style Mandarino covers the details of presentations, hand and body movements for example, as well as the overarching questions every speaker should ask themselves, such as, why am I doing this in the first place. Someday you will face an audience. Get this book."

— Jeffrey Salmon, former Senior Speechwriter for
three U.S. Secretaries of Defense

"In this guide, Mandarino presents in an accessible and humorous style many great tips and tricks to improving your public speaking and communication skills. Whether you are a college student taking public speaking classes or a lawyer getting ready for trial, this book will help you to sharpen your skills to give the best and most engaging presentation possible."

— Temple Northup, Ph.D., Director, School of Journalism &
Media Studies, San Diego State University

Fearless Captivating Unstoppable

Your Guide to Better Communication and Public Speaking

Cobey Mandarino

dedicated to my mom

CONTENTS

PART TWO: THE ZONE

PART FIVE: YOU

INTRODUCTION

Picture yourself standing onstage under the blazingly hot midday sun. Fifteen thousand people are staring at you, waiting for you to say something brilliant. And if you fail to be exceptionally eloquent, your audience will not only start to jeer and stomp their feet, they'll also begin hurling fruit in your direction. Did I mention you're only covered in an embarrassingly scant linen sheet to keep people from seeing your nether regions? This is, without hyperbole, what the ancient Greeks had to endure when speaking in front of an audience.

Though you probably don't have to deal with such extreme circumstances, it doesn't make your anxiety any less legitimate. Everything in life is relative, and nerves are nerves, no matter how you slice it. But since you don't actually have to deal with dodging airborne tomatoes, you get the luxury of addressing some key ingredients that can make subduing your angst a little easier.

Allow me to share my own story about coping with stage fright.

I was in the fledgling stages of my acting career and found myself performing onstage with Alec Baldwin in the world's most competitive and intimidating city, New York. Nearly one thousand audience members at the American Airlines Theatre were eagerly staring at us, waiting to be entertained. I had waited my entire career for this incredible moment, and though I was thrilled beyond belief at this amazing opportunity, I was also scared out of my friggin' mind. What if I screw up and ruin everything for Mr. Baldwin and the rest of the cast? What if I flub a line and all those people start laughing at me? What if I'm so awful, the theatre company decides to never hire me again?

So, there you have it, you're not alone. Even someone who makes their living out of helping people speak in front of audiences has dealt with performance anxiety. In fact, this phenomenon effects millions of people, in all kinds of circumstances. Not only have you and I experienced this, but so has business magnate Warren Buffet, singer Adele, and actor Bill Hader. These are individuals whose actual job is to be the center of attention in front of enormous audiences with high expectations. And yet, they, and many others like them, have still had to cope with stage fright.

The list of potential remedies for this problem is extensive. Clients have told me they've turned to therapists, Xanax, and even whiskey to help them overcome their fear of speaking in front of people. And though therapy may help you decipher the root of the problem, there's still no guarantee you'll cure yourself of the issue. And I certainly don't recommend you use drugs to mask the problem.

I'm going to disclose something to you before you read any further. This book is not about overcoming performance anxiety. Not directly, at least. That's because there is no silver bullet or magic pill that cures it. If someone tells you there is, you should probably run — unless they're prescribing you drugs, they're misleading you.

This book is, instead, designed to teach you the foundational elements of communication that will help you develop into a powerful speaker. It is through mastering these principles that you will find yourself to be supremely confident every time you speak to an audience, big or small.

Think of it this way: no matter how beautiful your house may be, if you have a weak foundation, the structure will eventually crumble. However, if you put the effort into building a solid infrastructure, that same house will be stable and secure. It will stand strong, no matter the formidable conditions.

Likewise, if you pay attention to the fundamentals described in the following pages, I can assure you that you'll feel more confident in your ability to communicate than you ever have before. And with this sense of security, your fear will naturally begin to dissipate. The unease and apprehension will have less real estate to occupy. It will get boxed out by your composure and self-assurance.

When you devote your energy toward laying some essential groundwork, you'll spend more time feeling excited about your ability to communicate with skill and confidence. And, ultimately, you'll squander less time noticing your sweaty palms.

I know this to be true because I've experienced it firsthand. While I was nervously standing on that stage with Mr. Baldwin, I took a deep breath and reminded myself that I had all the necessary tools to handle anything that came my way. I was fully prepared, and absolutely clear about my goals. Instantly, my heart rate slowed and my mind stopped racing. I began to feel excitement *and* peace of mind. I was about to perform in front of a huge theatre full of people, and I was poised and ready to go.

For years as an acting coach, I used a similar approach to teach performers to feel that same sense of confidence. Now I'm doing it for all types of speakers, regardless of their profession. I have a passionate desire to share my methods outside of the theatrical world in order to help people of all walks of life feel tremendously excited about communicating. I'm confident this book will allow you to feel the same.

One final note before you dive in. This book is intended for speakers of all kinds, with audiences of all varieties. When I use a phrase such as "lecture hall," feel free to exchange it with "my supervisor's office" or "my client's 5th tee shot."

Cobey Mandarino

When I say "audience," understand that I mean "your hardworking employees," "your faithful podcast listeners," or even "that huge group of people staring at you with anticipation at your next TEDx Talk." It's all applicable, no matter the circumstances. Connection is connection, presence is presence, and confidence is confidence. Enjoy!

PART ONE: PREPARATION

It Ain't About You

THE IMPORTANCE OF KNOWING YOUR AUDIENCE

One of the deepest principles of life and leadership: it's not about you.
— Ken Blanchard

Those ancient Greeks knew what they were doing when it came to performing in front of critical audiences. All modern performance is rooted in what those visionary Athenians did some 2,500 years ago. And, like it or not, when you're speaking to your boss, a client, or a roomful of peers, you are performing. Every interaction you have is a characterization, and enactment, of how you feel about a certain subject and the people you are delivering it to.

Ask yourself these questions: "How do I behave around my supervisor?" "Is it different than the way I talk to my best friend?" "How about my parents?" You may even find that the way you speak to your mother is vastly different than how you talk to your father. All of this "mask work" you're doing is accomplished, for the most part, unconsciously. You don't have to think about the "costume changes" that are taking place. They just happen because it's second nature by this point.

That doesn't mean you *can't* consciously think about it. In fact, whenever the opportunity to speak to others is important to you, it's imperative you consider your audience before you utter even a single word. The more cognizant you are of who your audience is and what they want, the more you can sculpt your message in order to facilitate the most mutually profitable outcome.

The ideal of ancient Greek theatre was to investigate the inner self while simultaneously teaching the audience about the world around them. Modern-day communication can be seen through that same lens. Every interaction you have is an opportunity to be fully engaged with both your inner self and your listener, thus allowing you to teach and learn at the same time. In order for the Greeks to accomplish this, they needed to study the world around them. And by doing that, they knew the character and composition of their audience and what was needed to inform, educate, and entertain them.

When preparing for a meeting, pitch, or presentation, make sure you know your audience as well as the Greeks did and tailor your preparation accordingly. Ask yourself, "Who am I speaking to and what do they want to get out of this?" Ultimately, your goal is to help the people you're addressing leave the room more informed than when they came in. This is done by judiciously studying your audience and knowing exactly their bottom-line desire. Far too often speakers put too much focus on themselves and their marvelous content, and not enough on their audience. But you can't truly know what your content should be without a deep understanding of your audience. Remember, your listeners want to feel cared for and understood. The more you can decipher exactly who they are and what they want, the more you can accomplish that. And the more you identify who they are at their core, the more apt they are to listen to what you have to say.

Make sure you also know what level of understanding your audience is at. You don't want to waste their time with information they already know, nor do you want to confuse them with ideas they're not ready for. Even if you're giving the same presentation or pitch to two separate audiences, take the time to customize things accordingly. As an elementary example, the toast you'd give about your best friend at their bachelor/bachelorette party would be quite a bit different than the one you'd give at their wedding. Same person and subject, immensely different audience and delivery.

Wait, Why Am I Here Again?

THE OBJECTIVE BEHIND YOUR MESSAGE IS EVERYTHING

If you can't explain it simply, you don't understand it well enough.
— Albert Einstein

Once you know explicitly who your audience is, it's time to forge and fine-tune the intention behind your message. You need to know exactly what you want your listeners to take away after they've spent their valuable time with you. A strong objective/intention gives you a goal to passionately strive toward, and will be your driving force as you communicate. It offers you clear direction and will bring your message to life. Without this goal, you'll meander, and your listeners' minds will as well.

For many years while living in Seattle, the Microsoft Corporation essentially paid my bills. I was a spokesperson, actor, and voiceover artist for them — speaking at events, and performing in commercials and corporate videos. One of the main reasons I was fortunate enough to be hired by them so consistently was because I was able to take direction, thread it into an objective, and put it into actionable behavior. I knew how to determine and understand their brand's message and then convey it clearly to their customers.

When you're doing gig work for a multi-billion dollar corporation such as Microsoft, it's important to understand that time is money. The team that hires you wants to feel at ease knowing you can work efficiently and effectively. They need to feel secure that when they explain to you the goal of the project, you'll be able to swiftly put that into action in a powerfully effective manner. Microsoft has thousands of employees who are constantly crafting and tweaking their company's goals and objectives. They are experts at it and they want the consultants they hire to be as well. Strong marketing objectives are a huge reason they, and many companies like them, are so incredibly successful.

I encourage my clients to take the same approach I did as an actor when they're developing their pitch or presentation. I make sure they understand that the most important thing they need to focus on when preparing, in tandem with their audience, is their objective. Even a one-on-one conversation with a colleague is remarkably more powerful with an intentional message than without one. Robust intentions give you a goal to work toward, and help direct purpose and effort. They stimulate focus, energy, and action and lead to illuminating discovery.

While preparing, set a strong objective based on the needs of your audience, and point your presentation directly toward that goal. Write it down and then keep questioning the potential impact of it. Share it with friends and colleagues and then tweak and sharpen it until there's no question in your mind that it is absolutely bulletproof. Objectives are the driving forces behind everything we do as human beings. They should also be the primary impetus behind your message.

Poets and Thieves

WHY YOU SHOULD STUDY THE GREATS

Every artist is a cannibal, every poet is a thief.

—- Bono

When I first started performing I was thoroughly captivated by the work of actor Gary Oldman. I was fascinated by his complexity and his willingness to take bold and dynamic risks during his performances. So, I studied him frequently. I watched every film he was in and was determined to figure out what made him tick as a performer. I viewed this process as if it were a mathematical equation I could figure out if I spent enough time studying the data. I studied his voice, mannerisms, and technique in an attempt to get to the root of his artistic choices and looked for roles that allowed me to put those observations into action.

I am absolutely a firm believer that you need to bring your own unique perspective into everything you do. However, I also believe that every good poet is a bit of a pirate. In other words, inspiration can lead you to originality. I learned an incredible amount from studying Mr. Oldman, which allowed me to develop into my own distinctive artist.

Likewise, studying and learning from accomplished speakers offers one of the best ways for you to learn and grow as a presenter. There's an abundance of recordings of great speakers on YouTube — from TEDx Talks to great presidential speeches. When you watch their delivery, take note of everything they do. Observe their vocal patterns, body language, and their use of silence. You'll invariably find their performances to be open, inviting, and strong. They use their physicality in ways that accentuate their key points. They will vary their vocal tone, and intelligently use pitch, volume, and timbre to their advantage. There will be little extraneous fidgeting and you'll notice how grounded they are. Pay close attention to how certain speakers utilize pace. Great communicators take their time and deliver their words with strong intention. They use silence as a tool to allow points to land and to keep their audience engaged.

The most important thing you'll want to keep an eye on is how much of their authentic personality shows when they speak. Observe how they use their persona and openness to help convey their own unique perspective. It's this approach that allows great speakers to stand out among a sea of other people who are equipped with the same exact knowledge.

Ten Out of Ten Free Throws Made

PRACTICE MAKES PROFICIENCY

Practice is the best of all instructors.

—- Publilius Syrus

In 2008, Malcolm Gladwell came out with the *New York Times* bestselling book, *Outliers: The Story of Success*. In it, he unearths what he believes to be the reason for why certain people have achieved such profound success. He frequently shares his theory of the "10,000 hour rule," which essentially states that it takes 10,000 hours of practice to become an expert at any one thing. Gladwell writes, "Research suggests that once a musician has enough ability to get into a top music school, the thing that distinguishes one performer from another is how hard he or she works. That's it."[1]

Michael Jordan, one of the best and most successful athletes of all time, shot 1,000 jump shots a day in practice. If you're wondering if that's a lot, just ask yourself when was the last

---

[1] Gladwell, Malcolm. 2008. *Outliers: The Story of Success*. Little, Brown and Company.

time you did 1,000 of anything in a day. Jordan was, of course, an exceptionally gifted athlete. But if that was all it took to be the best of all time, he wouldn't have bothered with all of that repetition. The thing about practice is that it makes your "game day" so much smoother and easier. The situations Jordan faced on the court were handled with aplomb because he had drilled through them time and time again.

The same thing can be said for your pitch or presentation. The more you know it like the back of your hand, the more you will be able to handle obstacles with ease because you're so familiar with the subject matter. Do you need to practice your speech 1,000 times a day? Of course not. It's up to you how much work you want to put into your project. You don't have to carry the desire to be the Michael Jordan of TED Talks to understand that the more work you put in, the more rewards you get out.

Malcolm Gladwell and Michael Jordan are clearly both aware of the adage "Practice makes perfect." When it comes to communication, I prefer to rephrase it: "Practice makes proficiency." Nothing will make you more confident, comfortable, and at ease than practicing your speaking skills. Conversely, there's not much that will make you feel more nervous than being underprepared. In the case of a presentation, each time you practice it on your own you'll become more comfortable. You'll begin to know your material inside and out, elevating your confidence for when you deliver it to an actual audience. You'll also start to figure out the structure and rhythm, and things will begin to feel like second nature.

Try to take advantage of any opportunity to practice your speaking skills, whether it be with friends or an employee at the grocery store. Study yourself while you speak. Notice how much eye contact you make, how many filler words (see Chapter 42) you use, and how present you are during the conversation. In the case of a specific pitch or presentation, try practicing it several different ways to see if you can unearth something impactful you might not have otherwise. Once you know what you're saying comprehensively, you'll be able to throw it away a bit and intelligently improvise in front of your listeners.

Why You're Putting Everyone to Sleep

HOW YOUR VOICE CAN MAKE
OR BREAK YOUR DELIVERY

It was the kind of voice that the ear follows up and down, as if each speech is an arrangement of notes that will never be played again.

— F. Scott Fitzgerald

What if every time you turned on Spotify, or your satellite radio, the singer's voice stayed on the same exact note throughout the duration of the song? My guess is you'd stop listening to music altogether, except maybe to help you fall asleep. There's a reason a singer's voice changes pitch throughout a song — it's more interesting, dynamic, and pleasing to the ear.

Monotone voices essentially have the effect of a hypnotist's swaying watch. They put people to sleep. When you alter your pitch while speaking, however, you're sending a message to your listeners' minds to stay awake. It's an incredibly valuable technique to use, particularly when you've reached a point in your talk that you feel is crucial for people to hear.

Research shows that listeners tend to absorb only a fraction of what another person says.[2] The majority of what they are absorbing is the speaker's tone of voice and their body language. So, oftentimes, it's less about what you say than how you say it. Your content may be top-notch, but unless it's delivered in a vocally interesting way, many folks will check out. It's more challenging for an audience to maintain concentration when a speaker uses a characterless, vanilla voice. Vocal flatness is uninspiring and, after a while, many listeners will stop paying attention altogether.

Tone, volume, pitch, and timbre all add layers of nuance to the information you're offering and help keep the audience fully engaged from beginning to end. Practice vocal variety in your everyday life so that it feels more natural to you. Notice the things that capture the attention of your listener and keep sharpening that on a regular basis. You'll be pleasantly surprised at how people will prick up their ears when you add vocal variety in your delivery.

Another important element to pay close attention to is the pattern of your voice. I've had many clients who are terrific wordsmiths but were unaware of how their vocal patterns were weakening their message. One detrimental habit I encounter with clients is sentences ending with an upward

---

[2] Mehrabian, A. 1972. *Nonverbal Communication*. Transaction Publishers.

inflection, as if the speaker is asking a question with every-thing they say. This puts doubt in the listener's ears and mind. Without being consciously aware of it, your audience will lack trust in your message because the pattern of your voice suggests uncertainty. Recording yourself (discussed in the next chapter) is a great way to catch these vocal tendencies.

Watching You Watching Me

GET AHEAD BY
RECORDING YOURSELF

Formal education will make you a living;
self-education will make you a fortune.

— Jim Rohn

When I first started speaking professionally, I found it very difficult to watch recordings of myself. I was incredibly self-critical. It's one of the drawbacks of having perfectionist tendencies. I even found it challenging to simply listen to my voice on audio recordings. Who is this unrecognizable person speaking? Why do they sound so strange? I often felt like I barely recognized myself. Fortunately, I got over this, which allowed me to make great strides in my progress as a performer and speaker.

Recording myself was one of the best tools I added to my repertoire. I made it a habit to do this before letting anyone see my performances. I wanted to make sure I covered every detail possible before I would practice with an out-side eye. This way, when I did rehearse in front of friends or colleagues, they could focus on the finer points of my message. They didn't need to waste time correcting the more obvious things I was able to catch as a result of studying myself.

It takes a while to get accustomed to watching recordings of yourself, but it can be invaluable in helping you improve your skills. All of those habits people have pointed out to you (or have been reluctant to point out) become starkly illuminated. Once you start to notice them yourself, you'll be eager to make swift adjustments. It truly serves as one of the best motivators. All that needless pacing you've been doing will turn into a strong, grounded presence. Those "ums" and "uhs" you've been inclined to needlessly throw in will quickly start to disappear. Your inability to make eye contact with people will shift into a confident ability to directly address your audience.

This type of exercise can all be accomplished via the video application on your smartphone. However, you can also glean a considerable amount from a simple audio recording. As mentioned before, you might find this task excruciating at first. But that's part of the purpose of this exercise. The more you recognize your habits, traps, and deficiencies, the more you can improve upon those things. It's a terrific way to recognize how you might come across to an audience. When you record yourself speaking and then watch it back, you may observe yourself doing things you didn't even realize. This provides you with the opportunity to adjust these issues before stepping in front of an actual audience.

One caveat: make sure you're not relying solely on your own analysis. Your viewpoint is going to be somewhat biased, and so it's impossible to be completely objective about yourself. Communicate with others to see if what you're observing is what they're also noticing. The more those things line up, the more you can start to trust your own critique.

Hey, Can I Ask a Favor?

GET FEEDBACK FROM FRIENDS AND COLLEAGUES

Accept both compliments and criticism.
It takes both sun and rain for a flower to grow.

—- Unknown

While practicing on your own can be quite fruitful, it's typically even better to do it in front of another set of eyes. Even if that person is simply your partner, a sibling, or a friend. For starters, they're going to have a more impartial point of view. As mentioned in the previous chapter, it's essentially impossible to critique yourself and not be biased. That's not to say a friend can't be partisan, but they'll at least have an alternative perspective. At the bare minimum, it gives you a chance to practice your craft and get used to speaking in front of a live human.

Additionally, the feedback you receive might turn out to be quite useful. In fact, it could actually stimulate a conversation that will lead to a few invaluable discoveries. Ask your test audience about your pace, your body language, and if your ideas were clear. Was there anything that confused them? What elements might help you improve your message?

Sometimes getting feedback from others can be a greater challenge than watching recordings of ourselves. Particularly for those of us with strong imaginations and even stronger wills. In general, most people want to feel like their talents are appreciated. Criticism can be a hard pill to swallow, especially with something we already feel vulnerable about.

One of the most important things I've learned is to be open to others' opinions of my abilities. If viewed through the lens of skill advancement, this can be a tremendous gift. Earlier in my career, I had a tendency toward being a bit stubborn and reluctant to accept constructive criticism. Over time, however, I began to realize the importance of accepting valuable appraisals of my work. Not only was it profitable, it was also incredibly liberating to let go of the futile desire to be flawless all the time.

Stop Looking at Me,
I'm Trying to Concentrate

DISTRACT YOURSELF IN PRIVATE SO IT DOESN'T BOTHER YOU IN PUBLIC

Don't blame the distractions. Improve your focus.

— Unknown

I'm a big believer in the power of meditation and have been practicing it for nearly twenty years. Therefore, one might think distractions aren't an issue for me. But, unwelcome noises, visual intrusions, and even strong smells can sometimes throw me off my game. I have to consistently work on my ability to focus.

In my early thirties I was speaking to a small, yet distinguished, audience in New York City, and was eagerly anticipating the event to be a big stepping stone for me. There is something about the cocktail of youth, ambition, and the Big Apple that can turn you into a nervous wreck as you attempt to impress people and move up the career ladder. Early on in this particular evening, I noticed someone I recognized as a pillar in the industry, and found myself frequently checking in on him as a barometer for how I was doing. It was not the best decision. From the very start, I noticed him with his elbow on the armrest of the chair, and his chin in his hand. He appeared bored, and that only increased my unease.

Fortunately, I was able to make it through the evening without any major hiccups or gaffes. However, I probably subtracted five years off my life due to the anxiety of letting that one individual shape how I felt.

Following the event, there was a cocktail hour at a nearby bar. I was surprised to see that key player whom I thought would have hurried home as soon as the lights came up. After some time, we eventually spoke. I had resigned myself to hearing him tell me how poorly I had performed. I was stunned, however, when the first words out of his mouth were "That was terrific." I couldn't believe what I was hearing. The same person who had looked like he was on the verge of taking a nap while I was onstage was declaring how much he enjoyed himself. We spoke for quite a while, and I couldn't help but mention that his body language made me think he wasn't listening to me at all. His reply was simple and straightforward. It was so much more benign than the story I had created in my head while I was onstage. He plainly said, "Oh, I always sit like that because it's more comfortable."

There I was, unnecessarily torturing myself because of someone's posture. He wasn't doing anything extreme. There were no dirty looks, no passive-aggressive sighs. He was simply resting his head. All of that worrying for nothing. Had I simply noticed it and quickly let it go, I would have been able to actually enjoy myself.

There are going to be distractions when you speak. And the bigger your audience, the greater the chance you're going to have one, or perhaps several. Once you know your content thoroughly, start throwing some diversions in your path while you work on your delivery. Turn on the television, practice while you're doing something else so you're forced to multi-task, or even tell a friend shoot you disinterested looks. Once you can do all of this without being thrown off, you'll be more than ready to ignore that person resting their chin in their palm.

Do This, Don't Do That

WHAT YOU SHOULD AND SHOULD NOT MEMORIZE

Starting strong is good. Finishing strong is epic.

—- Robin Sharma

You absolutely should be extremely familiar with what you're going to say during your meeting, presentation, or pitch before you're in front of an audience. However, you don't want to sound like a robot, mindlessly reciting a series of canned words. I typically encourage my clients not to memorize everything or recite things by rote. It merely locks you into one way of delivering things. And if that one method escapes your mind, you're up the creek. Ultimately, you want to be well-versed while also sounding as natural and spontaneous as possible.

A great way to feel like you're starting on the right foot and ending on a similarly solid note, though, is by memorizing the opening and closing sections of your presentation. The goal is to make certain you start out strong, which sets you up for having confidence throughout the rest of your meeting or presentation. Likewise, if you finish adeptly, it will ensure your audience departs while you're on solid footing. Having these two anchors will help frame your content in a way that sets you up for success.

It can also be very useful to memorize certain sections you feel are exceptionally important. Find those moments in your delivery that are essential and that your listeners absolutely cannot miss. Then, learn them cold. Write them out, say them out loud, and retool them so they're exactly how you want your audience to digest them. Doing this will provide you with moments throughout your pitch when you can securely tether yourself if needed.

The most critical thing you'll want to memorize is the order and structure of your ideas. Write things in outline form and learn that summary impeccably. Just make sure you're able to deliver it in several different ways. Practice improvising sections over and over and change it up every time. This way, when you get a little lost, all you have to do is take a quick peek at your notes, find your spot, and begin again. You'll be so adept at handling each section in different ways that it won't matter how wayward you might become.

Get Your Ish Together

IT'S TIME TO GET ORGANIZED

For every minute spent organizing, an hour is earned.
—- Benjamin Franklin

Often the focus of advice regarding public speaking is primarily about how you perform once you're in front of an audience. Without question, that's a very important part of the equation. However, before you even get in front of an audience, you need to spend a great deal of time researching and outlining what it is you're going to say. You may have exceptional presentation skills, but if your content and structure are all over the map, people aren't going to retain what you told them.

Once you've chosen a simple and clear objective, structure your presentation around that target. If you stray from your message too often and go on too many tangents, you'll lose your audience's attention. Create an outline based around your central theme and write down supporting evidence and examples. Having a rock-solid theme thoroughly fleshed out will make it that much easier to stay on point during your presentation. This will, in turn, allow your audience to leave with that singularly compelling takeaway.

As mentioned earlier, you want to be able to envision your entire presentation in outline form. It's sort of the opposite of writing a book. Instead of starting with an outline and then building it into something longer and more detailed, you want to do the reverse. Write down all of the specifics, then work on simplifying things. Keep trimming the fat so you can get to a place where you can see the bullet points in your head.

The other benefit of working this way is that the more you work on consolidating, the more you'll start to know your delivery implicitly. Once you have everything down to its most minimal form, start improvising each section out loud. Try it one way and then look at things from a different perspective and try it another. Rinse and repeat. Get your mental outline trimmed down to the most essential elements. You want to keep things simple enough that you can remember everything without ever needing your notes. Before you know it, you'll be so comfortable with your subject material, you'll be winging things in your sleep.

Pythagoras Had It Right

THE SIGNIFICANCE OF
THE NUMBER THREE

The soul of a man is divided into three parts, intelligence, reason, and passion. Intelligence and passion are possessed by other animals, but reason by man alone.

— Pythagoras

The number three has always had great significance. The Greek philosopher Pythagoras even postulated that it was the perfect number, representing beginning, middle, and end. Whenever you're speaking to an audience, you must keep in mind their capacity for recalling information. Breaking down your message into three distinct modules allows your audience to absorb the data you're giving them in easily digestible slices.

The three part list I often work with: 1) Personal Anecdote; 2) Problem; 3) Solution.

I'm a strong believer in starting things out with a personal anecdote because it helps draw your listeners in. Anyone can recite an assortment of facts that are, nowadays, readily available online. But, only *you* have access to what it's like to have lived your life. It's what sets you apart and makes you unique, and utilizing this personalization will go a long way in making listeners want to tune in to what you have to say. Once you've identified how you and your message intertwine, ask yourself how a personal anecdote might relate to the subject you're presenting. Then, go one step further and ascertain how your personal relationship to the material might be similar to that of your audience.

The second phase is to present the problem. Your audience has an obstacle they need to work around, and you're there to identify and solve it. It's the reason you're speaking to them in the first place. Remember to keep it tied in with how this effects you personally, and also how it has, or possibly will, effect your listeners.

Finally, present them with the grand solution. Explain to them the formula that delivers you and your audience to a more advantageous status. Not only do you need to solve the problem that has been identified, you also want to tie it back in with your original anecdote. Again, make sure it applies directly to you *and* your listeners. You want them to feel confident this solution is not only going to solve their problem, but will also improve their personal or professional life in the process.

Let's Get Visual

HOW TO USE VISUAL AIDES AND HOW NOT TO USE VISUAL AIDES

Visuals express ideas in a snackable manner.

— Kim Garst

If the notion of having all eyes on you scares you to death, visual prompts can be an effective way to briefly redirect the audience's attention. Furthermore, they can allow you to support your message in an even stronger way. These visuals can be by way of an image, a graph, or simply an impactful phrase displayed on screen.

Make absolutely certain that whatever you use, it not only enables you to feel more comfortable with your presentation, it also allows your audience to better understand your message. It is typically a good idea to prepare the first draft of your presentation without any visuals, then return to your content to see where slides are truly helpful. This will ensure that you do not distract your audience from your bottom line, and that each visual will be legitimately useful.

Photos, diagrams, and short videos are great tools to help supplement your message. Don't be afraid to have fun with it. The more fun you have putting it together, the better chance your audience will have fun along with you.

One trap to watch out for, though, is getting too caught up in your accompanying aides.

Early in my career I taught yoga to help supplement my income. I took great pleasure in teaching this physical, yet extremely mindful, practice. I also truly enjoyed putting music playlists together to help complement the pose sequences I was leading my students through. Yogis would often remark quite positively on the songs I chose. For better or worse, I started to develop a bit of a reputation as "the teacher with the great playlists."

I began to realize, however, that some of my newer students were being introduced to my classes often because of word of mouth about my song selections. I started to recognize there was an expectation about the music which was superseding the reason I wanted to teach in the first place. It was becoming too much about the auditory elements of my class and not enough about the physical and emotional benefits that had originally inspired me to teach.

Understanding this, I started to withdraw my attention to the music significantly. I wanted to get back to my roots to see if, ultimately, it made for a better overall experience. Occasionally, I would get a comment from a student asking why I no longer used music in my classes. The vast majority, however, enjoyed the more stripped-down version of my approach.

I discovered that my playlists had become an unnecessary crutch. They were actually doing me and my students a disservice. They were distracting me from the essential purpose of yoga, which is to rid yourself of those types of distractions so you can see what's truly going on internally. By dropping the music and focusing on the more nuanced parts of the practice, I was able to offer a more well-rounded, deeper experience. I was then able to sprinkle in the occasional song to help *support* the asana practice, rather than be the focus of it.

I mention this to make a comparable point. How often have you witnessed a presentation where it was obvious that great attention went into creating the slides, but very little into how they were being utilized?

To avoid the pitfall of "Death by PowerPoint," make sure you understand that slides are simply a visual aid to help support what you're communicating to your audience. No matter how good your slides are, if they take center stage, the presentation will most certainly be less effective than if you, your message, and your audience are the main areas of focus. Keep your visuals simple and supportive, and always remember that the greatest visual aid is you. Your audience is there to hear what you have to say because they trust you have something invaluable to offer. They want to see you, hear your words, and observe your body language in order to better understand and evaluate your content and inspirations. By all means, use slides, but make sure they're *accompanying* your presentation, not *controlling* it. Use them as visual complements to your words and as a tool to emphasize your message.

Cheat Sheets

HOW TO USE NOTES

I wisely started with a map.

— J. R. R. Tolkien

One of the biggest fears people have when speaking is that suddenly, out of nowhere, their mind will go blank. They'll have absolutely no idea what comes next and end up feeling absentminded and embarrassed. Documenting all of your key points on index cards is a perfectly acceptable safety device to help you avoid this. Don't be afraid to utilize them. This method is especially useful if public speaking makes you anxious and you're worried you won't remember anything you've prepared.

Much like your visual aides, however, make certain you have them only as a safety tool and you're not dependent on them. Staring at your notes will make you appear disingenuous and you'll end up losing your audience. Keep your notes as minimal as possible and use only brief prompts for each topic you'll be discussing. Oftentimes, simply knowing you have them with you is enough to prevent you from needing them.

If you are going to use hard copy notes as opposed to something digital, make sure they look clean and professional. Stay away from spiral-bound notepaper or tattered journals that could become the unintended star of the show. Make sure there's nothing written on the flip side of the page you're reading from so that it's not a distraction to the audience. And never hold the cards between your face and the people you're talking to. The rule of thumb is, if you can't see your audience, they can't see you. Hold your notes informally at about chest height so you can utilize them easily without having to lift and lower them repeatedly from your side. If you're using notes quite frequently, it can be distracting to watch someone's arm yo-yo up and down. It's a surefire way to have people paying more attention to your oscillating arm than your message.

If you do decide to use notes, resist any temptation to read your entire presentation word for word from them. Notes can be useful, but, like PowerPoint, they can also become a crutch if you're not careful. If you're still working up to going note-free, keep it as minimal as possible. Ultimately, notes draw your eyes down and force everyone to stare at the top of your head. That's a certain way to lose your audience's attention quickly. Use notes that are small and unobtrusive such as index cards with just a few key words to keep you on topic. Keeping things minimalistic will allow you to stay on track without tempting you to read your entire message from a page. The most important thing when speaking is that you're making eye contact, maintaining a sincere delivery, and genuinely connecting with your audience.

PART TWO: THE ZONE

Drinking on the Job

WHY HYDRATING IS SO IMPORTANT

There's nothing more beautiful than the way the ocean refuses to stop kissing the shoreline, no matter how many times it's sent away.
— Sarah Kay

There are so many great TEDx videos out there to be viewed. I see an incredible amount of good content and am inspired by the amount of talent and intelligence there is out there. However, I'd approximate that three-quarters of the speakers I watch have a pronounced, and most likely self-induced, dehydration problem. Because of this, I become so distracted by the sound of smacking gums that I find it hard to pay attention to what they're actually saying. Some of this, of course, is nerves. When you experience anxiety, your body may shift fluids from your mouth to other parts of your body. This fight-or-flight response may cause you to have excess water in your sweat glands and not enough saliva in your mouth.

But this is only part of the reason your mouth feels like the Mojave. According to studies, 75 percent of Americans suffer from chronic dehydration.[3] This explains why I hear all those gums colliding when I listen to speakers give their presentations. One of the reasons it's so frustrating to me is that it's such an easy fix. Make sure you're adequately hydrated and this issue typically goes away. This doesn't mean that having a bottle of water onstage with you will solve all your problems. It's essential to hydrate *before* you speak. Not just the day of, but the day prior as well. There is no long-term, quick-fix for hydration.

You're probably already aware that being properly hydrated is essential to good health in general. If you're not drinking two to three Nalgene bottles worth of water a day currently, start doing it. Don't make the mistake of guzzling copious amounts of water right before you speak. You'll be spending your entire presentation wondering where the closest bathroom is, rather than the message you want to get across to your listeners.

That being said, there is nothing wrong with taking a sip of water in the middle of your presentation. Ideally, you'll want to do it during a transition moment. But if you're about to cough, or your mouth sounds like it's home to the Sahara Desert, by all means knock back a bit of that H_2O. This is another case where, if whatever is going on with

---

[3] Taylor, Kory & Jones, Elizabeth. 2022. Adult Dehydration. National Library of Medicine.

your voice is so distracting to your audience that they're not getting the message, you're doing yourself a disservice by pretending not to need it. Just make sure you're not at the well so often that your listeners start wondering how soon before you're sprinting to the bathroom.

Here are a few more reasons why water is essential for your well-being as a communicator: 1) It regulates your body temperature so you're not overheating during those intense engagements. 2) It protects your joints and allows you to stand for longer periods of time. 3) It creates saliva so you're not sounding parched with all the speaking you have to do during a meeting, pitch, presentation, or a simple conversation with a colleague. 4) It improves blood-oxygen circulation, allowing your brain to work more efficiently. 5) It boosts energy, something that's critical for those longer engagements with clients and colleagues. 6) It improves your mood and will keep you feeling positive when speaking to others.

The Eye of the Tiger

HOW SWEATING WILL GET YOU PAST YOUR MENTAL BLOCKS

Be stronger than your excuses.

— Unknown

It's easy to get frustrated when you're working on a new project or task and things aren't going as smoothly as you'd like. You might be making great progress and then suddenly come up against a hurdle that seems as big as the Great Wall of China. We're human and we all encounter obstacles sometimes. There can be many ways around this suspension in progress, but one that's extremely useful is to literally shake things up. You may need to simply get the blood flowing and work out some of the stress that's stored up in your body and mind. When my clients encounter adversities in their work, I encourage them to go for a run or bike ride or anything that gets their blood pumping. For starters, it gets your mind off the problem. Nothing will block your creative ideas more than fixating on something and not giving it room to breathe.

Working out before you have an important engagement can be incredibly useful as well. It's almost impossible to feel anxious after a good workout, so make time to exercise before you're in front of your supervisor or that group of potential investors. Exercising will help take your mind off the anxiety you might be feeling about being in front of an audience in the first place. Moving your body decreases muscle tension, which lowers your body's contribution to feeling mentally anxious. Furthermore, increasing your heart rate with exercise changes your brain chemistry. It increases the availability of essential anti-anxiety hormones and neurotransmitters, including serotonin, dopamine, and gamma aminobutyric acid (GABA).[4] Overall, exercising consistently builds up resources that bolster resilience against troubling emotions.

Working out is also a great time to practice what you'll be sharing with people. As mentioned in chapter 8, the more you're able to work through intrusions while you're practicing, the easier it will be to deal with obstacles when you're in front of your listeners.

---

[4] Lin, Tzu-Wei & Kuo, Yu-Min. 2013. Exercise Benefits Brain Function. National Library of Medicine.

You Think You're Better Than Pavarotti?

WHY YOU ABSOLUTELY MUST WARM UP YOUR VOICE

Too much time warming up and you might miss the race.
Don't warm up at all and you might not finish it.

—- Unknown

Professional athletes don't come running out of the locker room and immediately start playing a game. Similarly, musicians and singers don't hop out of bed and promptly start performing in front of an audience. Athletes stretch and run drills before they take on their opposition, while musicians and vocalists practice scales in order to warm up.

When it's "game time" for you, you should be warming up your voice as well. Vocal warmups stretch your vocal cords and increase the flow of blood to your larynx. They also get other essential body parts ready for speaking, including your face, lips, tongue, and lungs. Warming up properly will reduce raspiness and vocal lethargy when you're going to be using your voice over long stretches of time. It also allows you to utilize a wider range of pitch, which is essential for including vocal variety in your delivery.

One of the greatest tools I learned while in grad school was the Linklater Technique. It was developed by Scottish speech coach Kristin Linklater and popularized in her seminal book, *Freeing the Natural Voice*. The premise behind it is that we're born with a very free and unencumbered voice, but over time we develop certain protective blocks that stifle that natural sound.

Think of how uninhibited and vocal a young child can be. They experience a feeling and they simply let it out. They don't consider whether or not the sound is going to be pleasing to those around them. They express themselves purely and freely. Now trace a child's growth from infant to teen and note how the censoring filter grows with each year. Your parents, friends, and society all contribute to you tamping down your expression. It isn't acceptable in our society to say whatever is on your mind in whatever volume you see fit.

Of course, some of this is necessary. Can you imagine if everybody walked around sharing their every thought as loudly as they could at the grocery store or in a coffee shop? It would be maddening. Through this self-imposed restriction and censorship, however, we do lose a lot of our personal freedom of expression. Linklater created impactful vocal warmups that help you tap back into this primal version of yourself. Don't worry, these exercises won't make you holler expletives at your coworkers. But, it will help you express yourself in an honest and clear way. Do yourself a favor and pick up Ms. Linklater's book. Or, better yet, hire a vocal coach and turn your voice into the amazingly versatile instrument it was intended to be.

You Like Me! You Really Like Me!

REMEMBER, THE AUDIENCE
IS ON YOUR SIDE

We rise by lifting others.

—- Robert Ingersoll

One thing that took me a while to understand in my early years as a performer is that when you attend an audition, the people in the room really want you to succeed. In fact, they *need* you to prosper. They're relying on your talent and hard work to help carry their project.

Despite popular belief among many novice and insecure performers, it does the director/producers/investors absolutely no good for you to fail. They're praying you're the next Bradley Cooper or Cate Blanchett, because it ultimately makes their job that much easier. Whether it's a $10,000 or $10 million budget makes no difference. It's all relative, and an important project is an important project, no matter the price tag.

For many of you, speaking in front of an audience of 2, let alone 200, feels like one of the most daunting things on Earth. You're worried about failing, or you think you'll somehow be rejected or humiliated. The people worth connecting with, though, are invariably on your side and want you to succeed. If they're wise, they consider listening and learning to be an opportunity to leave the room smarter and better informed than when they came in. If you keep in mind that your listeners want you to do well, it makes the process of being the center of attention that much easier.

There is always the chance you'll have someone present who's in an irritable mood and can't be swayed. Let that be their problem. Even the most accomplished speaker in the world won't be able to win them over. Focus on the rest of the group that came to learn and are pulling for you to help them enrich their lives. Come prepared, stick to your message, speak from your heart, and you're certain to succeed.

Don't Be So Damn Hard on Yourself

HOW BEING TOO SELF-CRITICAL ENDS UP BACKFIRING

You will never speak to anyone more
than you speak to yourself, so be kind.

— Unknown

There are plenty of reasons why people are hard on themselves. Some of us simply have a desire for personal development and we think being self-critical is the best way to improve. I can certainly be guilty of this.

However, dissatisfaction with yourself doesn't necessarily help you move forward or achieve more in life. In reality it can make self-growth harder by creating unnecessary and insurmountable hurdles. This is because if you are always hard on yourself, you won't feel contentment when you do succeed, because you're so accustomed to being dissatisfied. Being relentlessly self-critical can cause a lot of stress, and it seldom benefits anyone.

Constant self-persecution can also get in the way of connecting with others, which is undoubtedly one of the most important elements of great communication. The more your attention is turned inward toward disappointment, the less bandwidth you'll have to relate to others. Keep in mind that everyone has bad days and less-than-ideal performances — even those high-level executives you're so determined to impress.

The more you do something, the better you're going to become at that thing. However, with this increase in frequency comes the potential for the occasional error. Mistakes are going to happen, but self-criticism about these errors can lead to poor judgment. One of these potentially bad decisions is the desire to cover things up. It can be terribly awkward watching someone try to pretend they haven't made a mistake. You can witness, in real-time, their face go from contentment to panic in mere seconds. It can be just as painful for the audience to watch as it is for the presenter to experience. As a result, it makes the mistake more pronounced and draws more attention to it.

One of my favorite things in life is the "happy accident." It's what happens when you make a mistake, roll with it, and something wonderful comes as a result.

I remember once making what could have been a terribly embarrassing gaffe in front of an audience of 2,000 people. I felt my body completely freeze up. In a split second I had the choice of fight, flight, or simply let go and see where things take me. For a moment my audience looked just as nervous as I felt. I could see the curiosity on their faces, wondering how I was going to handle it. Something instinctually told me to take a long pause, a deep breath, and simply smile in acknowledgment of what had just happened.

I felt the weight lift from my shoulders, and from the audience's as well. When I made that decision to give into the possibilities, I saw everyone's faces lighten. They began to smile with me. Then, together, we began to laugh. I leaned into it and so did they. It was one of those good laughs that feels genuinely cathartic. They weren't laughing at me, they were laughing in support of me. I could feel it.

It remains one of my favorite moments from being onstage. It also serves as a great lesson to not only be okay with mistakes, but to embrace them. A colleague approached me afterward and said, "Thank you for that." I asked her what she meant and she replied, "Thank you for reminding me that life doesn't always have to be so serious."

Sh*t Happens

HOW TO EXPECT THE BEST
BUT PREPARE FOR THE WORST

Sometimes the bad things that happen in our lives put us directly on the path to the best things that will ever happen to us.

— Nicole Reed

We can all acknowledge that mistakes are going to happen. You're going to say the wrong words. The PowerPoint display is going to be glitchy. Someone is going to have a coughing fit in the middle of the most important part of your delivery. You may or may not be able to laugh it off the way I did in front of all those people. What you absolutely can do, however, is be prepared for obstacles that might be thrown in your path. This way, when you do encounter them, you'll be able to handle things with ease.

One of the great advantages of preparing for the worst is, on the chance something challenging does come up, it won't feel so fatalistic. No doubt, to reach your aspirations you need an unflinchingly positive attitude, and a supreme belief that you can, and will, be great. However, another essential mindset is being prepared for obstacles that could potentially pop up during your quest for success.

This may seem like a cynical point of view. After all, aren't we supposed to have an undying belief we can achieve whatever we want, no matter what's in our way? The book *The Secret* will tell you that if you envision a positive outcome, it will undoubtedly happen. Well, if that were entirely true, we'd have a world chock-full of very wealthy, successful, and infallible people.

It's equally important to realize that we will, undoubtedly, come across challenges in everything we do. Including communicating with others. With a concrete plan in place, though, these hiccups can be overcome with much more ease and effortlessness. Prepping for the worst case scenario will make you feel grounded and prepared, and minimizes the fears and anxieties that can naturally surface when we're speaking in front of an intimidating audience.

So, prepare for questions that might otherwise throw you off. Have a colleague or friend ask you unscripted inquiries so that, on the day, you're ready to handle them. Wing your delivery without the PowerPoint, just in case you lose connectivity during your pitch. Have your husband or wife sigh, squirm, and even give you irritable looks to mimic that potential grump who shows up at the meeting. Think about the worst that could possibly happen, and then think about your most adept reaction. Doing this has the effect of minimizing fear, which can increase your composure come performance time.

It's Okay to Be Nervous

HOW ACKNOWLEDGING YOUR FEARS CAN ACTUALLY ALLEVIATE YOUR FEARS

Instead of fighting your anxiety, dance with it.
Welcome it. Relish it. It's a sign you're onto something.

— Unknown

Fear is an emotion that everyone experiences, yet rarely do people openly talk about it. That is because fear is far too often associated with weakness. A prevailing, yet groundless, thought is that if we acknowledge our nerves and/or fears, it conveys the message we are somehow inferior. That would equate to the ridiculous notion that *everyone* is inferior, because no one is completely impervious to it.

Generally speaking, denial is just a shortcut to getting stuck in the problem you find yourself in. However, one of the best ways to deal with your nerves is to acknowledge that you have them in the first place. So, get comfortable with your fear. Recognize it, acknowledge it, and figure out what you can learn from it. Tell a friend or colleague about it and see if, through discussion, you can figure out the root of the fear and become a stronger speaker because of this awareness.

Even the most accomplished public speaker can feel nervous in front of an intimidating audience. You see it often at the Academy Awards. A victorious actor steps up onstage, accepts their Oscar, and then heartily admits to the audience how nervous they are. These are professionals who are paid millions of dollars to perform confidently in front of the world, and yet they still encounter performance anxiety like the rest of us.

It happens to nearly everyone with a beating heart. There is something so disarming when people admit it to us, though. We see they are nervous and we hear it in their voice. But when they confess their nerves, it allows us all to breathe a little deeper. We feel the weight lift from the room, and from the speaker's shoulders as well. It works by letting everyone, collectively, off the hook.

Whether we're conscious of it or not, there is a common energy in any room full of people. You're constantly feeding off your listeners and they're feeding off you. The psychology of "mirroring" that you may have heard about alleges that one person's behavior subconsciously initiates the same behavior or attitude of another. So, if you can relieve the pressure your audience is feeling by acknowledging your own nerves, you'll likely reap the benefits as well.

My Bloody Lesson

KNOW YOUR SPACE / PLATFORM AND GIVE YOURSELF PLENTY OF TIME

By failing to prepare, you are preparing to fail.
—- Benjamin Franklin

One bit of fear you can nip in the bud right away is by making yourself familiar with the space or platform you'll be using so there is no mystery. Whether it be a meeting hall, a conference room, or Zoom meeting, you'll want to make sure you know the logistics comprehensively before you begin. Gather all of the information you can regarding the site, technical aspects, and allotted time. Having this information ahead of time will help you feel at ease when you're speaking, and gives you one less thing to worry about. The last thing you want is any unnecessary surprises that could throw you out of your rhythm and give you anxiety that you very easily could have avoided. Or even worse, cause you to miss the event altogether.

I was midway through a teaching semester where I had my process and equipment use down to almost a science. I knew exactly where the microphone was, I had the projector on the settings I preferred, and I could flip a switch and a giant screen would angelically lower from the rafters of the auditorium.

This all worked seamlessly until the one day I showed up to class just a few short minutes prior to the start time and found everything out of place. Another professor had used the room earlier and hadn't bothered to set things back to their usual home. I had to rush to get everything back where I needed it, all while my students were slowly trickling into the classroom.

To make matters more challenging, my students were typically eager to catch up with me prior to the start of class. Ordinarily, I really enjoyed this. However, on this particular day I needed to be quick and efficient in order to fit in everything I had structured into my lesson plan. My students didn't realize this, of course. One after another, my ambitious coeds came in wanting to chat while I feverishly attempted to get my ducks in a row.

Consequently, I was rushing, multitasking, and conversing, all of which resulted in me carelessly slicing my finger wide open on a sharp object. This sent blood streaming onto my clothes and the floor. I had essentially sliced a fairly large chunk of my pinky clean off.

Needless to say, I wasn't able to teach that day. Instead of making up lost time by rushing, I wound up wasting an entire day. As they say, haste makes waste. One of my favorite quotes is a gem that the Navy SEALs use: "Slow is smooth, and smooth is fast." It's invariably true. The slower you can go, the more efficient things tend to be. Conversely, the more you rush what you're doing, the more time you waste by making unnecessary mistakes.

I've always been a big proponent of knowing the room and the devices (e.g. microphone, projector, etc.) you'll be using before your engagement. This incident not only reaffirmed that, but also made me understand it never hurts to get to the venue early and check things again.

You Don't Have Time to Meditate, Because You Don't Meditate

HOW TO GET IN THE ZONE

*You should sit in meditation for twenty minutes a day,
unless you're too busy, then you should sit for an hour.*

— Zen Proverb

I could not be a bigger champion of the practice of meditation, regardless of whether you're preparing for a big event or not. It's been an absolute game changer for me, and I wouldn't be the same person today if not for my mindfulness practice.

I hear time and time again people declaring they don't have the time to meditate. This is, of course, nonsense. If it's important enough to you, you'll find the time. Before I started meditating regularly, I used the same excuse. I couldn't imagine devoting five minutes, much less an hour, of my day sitting in silence. Where was I supposed to find the extra time for that?

But, here's the wonderful thing about meditation. The more you do it, the more you become efficient at everything else in your life. You actually create more time because you become so much more clear-headed and productive in general. Problems resolve themselves quicker. Solutions come with less thought.

Another reason often served up for why people avoid meditation is that they don't have the focus for it. Their mind is too scattered. They find it challenging to sit for even five minutes because their monkey brain is briskly swinging from branch to branch. The point in meditating, however, is not to get your brain to stop thinking. It's to notice what your mind is actually doing. It's about being in the moment and observing your thoughts as if they were clouds passing overhead. It's about being present and aware. In doing this, your mind will consequently start to wander less. It's called a practice for a reason. The more you do it, the more adept you become at it.

Commit yourself to doing it five minutes a day for two weeks. Then increase that to ten over the next two weeks. Even if you meditate just fifteen minutes a day, you'll be reaping the rewards. Consequently, having this practice in your repertoire will make it easier to utilize prior to a big, nerve-racking event. Not only will you be sharper, you'll also be much calmer.

Because I have an established meditation practice, it's easy for me to sit and focus for ten or fifteen minutes before I get in front of an audience. I'm well aware, though, that meditation isn't everybody's cup of tea. Regardless of how you prepare, it's essential to take some time to get in the zone before you begin to speak. Find your version of getting focused and centered. Get some alone time, drink some water, listen to some calming music, and concentrate on your breathing.

Another terrific way to get focused is to repeat your objective to yourself. What key point do you want your audience to leave with? Find a specific and concise phrase that sums this up and use it as a mantra before you speak. If you are in front of an audience often, you may end up using a similar routine every time. This pattern will signal to your brain what you're about to do and will help trigger you into the right headspace. It might take some time to figure out the combination that suits you best, so be patient.

Some people find it necessary to mentally prepare the night before, others the morning of, and some in the moments immediately before they begin. If you're unsure where to start, think back to another time in your life when you were preparing for a pivotal occasion. What did you do before a piano recital, football game, or big test? See if those things help now, and modify until you find the right combination.

Whether it's meditation, taking a walk, or listening to music, find something that gets you primed, centered, and focused.

PART THREE: YOUR BODY AND VOICE

Breathe, Dammit!

HOW BREATHING PROPERLY IS THE MOST IMPORTANT THING YOU CAN DO TO PERFORM AT YOUR BEST

I've got to keep breathing. It'll be my worst business mistake if I don't.

— Steve Martin

If I had a dollar for every time someone underestimated the importance of proper breathing, I'd be an insanely wealthy man. It's a miracle cure when it comes to stress, and yet we still take it for granted. The mindfulness industry, which includes conscious breathing, is now a $1 billion line of business for a reason. Athletes, musicians, actors, and executives are all now understanding the importance of good breathing habits. Even the Navy SEALs (talk about a stressful job) spend copious amounts of time during their training working on, you guessed it, breathing. It's a crucial part of our existence. But, because we can do it both voluntarily and involuntarily, people often ignore the importance of practicing it.

Breathing is one of the most basic functions of the human body. Done correctly, it can help you sleep better, digest food more efficiently, improve your body's immune response, release powerful endorphins, and reduce stress levels. Every system in your body relies on oxygen. Breathing not only calms you down, it also gives you a greater sense of mental clarity. When you're anxious, your heart rate speeds up and your body goes into fight or flight. While your nervous system is in this state, the last thing it's trying to do is help you speak with clarity. It's simply looking for a way to get the hell out of the situation.

Breathing is typically the very first thing I work on with my clients. Doing it properly, according to very hard, scientific facts, will calm your nerves and allow you to work more efficiently.[5] My clients who embrace this knowledge from the start are invariably the ones who make the quickest progress. It's become an incredible prognosticator for me — better breathing equals a more relaxed mind and a better performance.

Download a breathing app and practice it every day. Or, better yet, take a yoga or meditation class. Then, when you start to feel your body tense up while speaking in front of people, you'll be able to take a moment to remind yourself

[5] Zaccaro, Andrea et al. 2018. How Breath-Control Can Change Your Life: A Systematic Review on Psycho-Physiological Correlates of Slow Breathing. National Library of Medicine.

to breathe deeply and properly. Your nervous system will know what to do next.

Understand that breathing properly is not something that happens overnight. You'll want to practice mindful breathing well before you're in front of an audience so it's easier to access this technique under pressure. If you don't practice slowing your breath down when the pressure is at bay, what do you think is going to happen when the stress dial gets cranked up several notches?

Why So Serious?

THE BENEFITS OF SMILING

If you see someone without a smile, give them one of yours.

— Dolly Parton

Numerous studies have shown that the act of seeing some-one else smile triggers an automatic muscular response that invites a smile on our own face.[6] That means science has actually proven that smiling is contagious. So ask yourself, would you rather have your listeners smiling back at you, or giving you a dull, indifferent look? If you answered the former rather than the latter, then you need to do yourself a big favor and smile in that meeting room.

Let me offer you another reason to smile when you're speaking to an audience. Picture this: you're at a party where you don't know anyone. Some folks are greeting you with a smile, some are ignoring you, and others are simply staring at you with no expression at all. Which group are you most likely to approach first? I'd be willing to bet it

---

[6] Spector, Nicole. 2018. Smiling can trick your brain into happiness - and boost your health. NBC News.

would be the ones who are sending that inviting smile your way. In most any situation, but particularly in those that make us feel uncertain or anxious, we are more willing to trust people who show us they are friendly and approachable. Therefore, the more you can disarm your audience with your smile, the more apt they are to listen and absorb what you have to say.

The other wonderful benefit of smiling is that it fires a signal back to your brain that you're happy. It triggers your reward system and activates joyful hormones and endorphins. It's good old-fashioned science. Psychologist and Harvard professor Amy Cuddy explains in her acclaimed TED Talk on body language that when your body takes on a joyful state, even artificially, your mind understands it as reality.[7] In other words, your nervous system doesn't know the difference between a pseudo smile and an authentic one. Therefore, as you trick your brain into thinking you're happy, you actually become happy. Psychosomatic science is pretty cool, isn't it?

Guess what happens when you get all those wonderful chemicals coursing through your veins. You become a better, more positive speaker. And it's not just you who benefits from this — your audience gets inspired too. They be-

---

[7] Cuddy, Amy. 2012. Your body language may shape who you are. TED. https://www.youtube.com/watch?v=Ks-_Mh1QhMc&t=26s

come happier, as a result. As I'm sure you can guess, happier people are more awake and willing to listen to what you have to say. It's a win-win scenario for everyone.

Feast Your Eyes on This

HOW EYE CONTACT CAN MAKE ALL THE DIFFERENCE

Worlds change when eyes meet.

—- Unknown

I was fresh out of college, living in New York City, and seeing a ton of live music on the weekends. It was one of my favorite things about living in the Big Apple. I saw an incredible number of bands over the years and, so, remember very few of them. There were a few groups that made it big, while most disappeared into the void, never to be heard from again.

There was one band in particular, however, that I'll never forget because of the enthralling stage presence of their front-woman. The band's music was very good. However, the X-factor that made the group so special was the charisma of their lead singer. She had extraordinary confidence onstage. And through that confidence she made remarkably direct, fearless eye contact with her audience members.

I remember vividly feeling like she was singing only to me. Her attention was audacious, yet also inviting. And she had perfect timing — she'd always make sure to move her attention to someone else before the eye contact became uncomfortably long.

I wasn't alone in feeling this way about her incredible performances. I'd speak to friends of both genders about her captivating presence, and invariably everyone would have the same response. She was the world champion of eye contact. Those particular shows were nearly twenty years ago and I still remember them vividly. It's a lesson in the power of eye contact I'll never forget.

Eye contact is crucial, whether you're performing in a band or speaking to people. Not just any eye contact will do, though. You need the right quantity *and* quality of visual attentiveness. We tend not to trust someone whose eyes are darting all over the place when we're communicating with them. But, likewise, stare unflinchingly at someone and you're bound to scare them off.

As the saying goes, the eyes are the window to the soul. What people are reading through your eyes is just as important as how much time you spend making eye contact with them. People can see your intention even if they're not consciously aware of it. This means that, especially in more intimate meetings, your audience may or may not buy into what you're telling them based on what they see in your eyes. Therefore, it's essential to have your audience's best interest in mind when you speak to them, because their internal lie detector will recognize it.

When communicating to a larger audience, make eye contact with as many people in the room as you can. Don't do it simply because you read in a communication book that it was a good practice. You need to make a *genuine* effort to spark a connection (see chapter 44) with one person before you decide to move on to the next. Speak as though you're communicating to an individual rather than a roomful of people. This will invoke intimacy and trust with your audience.

When your audience is smaller, it offers you a great opportunity to use this same method but on a more intimate scale. Share visual attention with each individual and allow yourself to be emotionally seen as you speak. And, perhaps most importantly, listen to your audience with your eyes (see chapter 31) so you can use those visual cues to help inform your delivery. If you're truly present, your audience will visually instruct you as to what you need to say or do next. Being energetically available to your colleagues goes a long way in winning them over. Conversely, there's not much worse than someone that is merely speaking at you, rather than to you.

I'm Sure What You're Saying Is Amazing but I Can't Understand You

---

THE IMPORTANCE OF ARTICULATION

If the tongue had not been framed for articulation,
man would still be a beast in the forest.

— Ralph Waldo Emerson

Great communication skills begin with a crisp and clear delivery. You may be able to generate beautiful words to express your thoughts and ideas, but if they aren't spoken in an articulate manner, they won't amount to much. Sharp technique is particularly essential when you speak to an audience that doesn't have the opportunity to ask questions or respond in any way. This is because your listeners don't have the aide of subtitles or a pause button at their disposal. Once a word or a sentence leaves your mouth, that may be your audience's one and only chance to absorb it. If a listener missed something you've said, they could potentially be missing out on the crux of your pitch. This can make or break your entire message. All that hard work and time devoted could potentially go for naught because you mumbled your way through a crucial moment.

If you want people to understand you, articulate each word cleanly and clearly. Being articulate, in general, is an essential business skill and is associated with competency and intelligence. People tend to refer to articulate speakers as "smart" and "trustworthy." The unfortunate truth is, many individuals miss out on key roles and promotions simply because they are unable to express their thoughts and ideas in a clear and articulate manner.

How many presidents can you remember who were mumblers? How about great TEDx speakers? Can you remember any that you admired despite the fact you couldn't make out what they were saying? Probably not. There's a reason that great speakers are, invariably, ones you can understand. I'm certain there are individuals out there who have potentially revolutionary messages that just aren't being heard on a global level because they can only manage to mutter their way through their delivery. It's a shame, because I'm sure we're missing a lot of great ideas from some incredibly intelligent individuals simply because we have a difficult time understanding their verbal execution.

So, practice being sharp and crisp on your consonants and make sure you're not muddling through anything you say on a day-to-day basis, even when you're speaking to a grocery store clerk or the salesperson at Home Depot. Try reading this chapter aloud a few times as a way to practice. The more you work on your articulation, the more it will come naturally to you. And the more articulate you are, the more powerful your words will be.

Your Mouth Is Saying Yes
but Your Body Is Saying No

WHY YOU NEED TO BE AWARE OF YOUR HAND GESTURES AND BODY LANGUAGE

*The most important thing in communication
is to hear what isn't being said.*

—- Peter Drucker

One of my favorite things to do when studying speakers is to observe their body language. I'm fascinated with movement, which is a big reason I got into teaching yoga years ago. I learned so much from watching the way a student entered the room or carried themselves throughout class. People say so much through the language of their gait and the hand gestures they use when they speak. Someone's upright posture or, conversely, their slumped carriage is sending a message to everyone around them. It's all deeply rooted in our moods and personalities.

While the secret to success in professional relationships frequently rests in your ability to verbally communicate effectively, it's often not your words but your nonverbal cues that are speaking the loudest. Body language is the use of physical expressions and mannerisms to communicate non-verbally, often done intuitively rather than intentionally. Whether you're doing it consciously or not, when you engage with others, you're constantly giving and receiving crucial physical messages. All of your wordless behaviors—your physical gestures, posture, tone of voice, and how much eye contact you make—send powerful signals. They can help you build trust, put your listeners at ease, and draw your audience toward you; or they can confuse, upset, and compromise what you're trying to convey.

In many circumstances, what comes out of your mouth and what you're conveying through your physical language may be two completely different messages. If you say one thing, but your physical signals are telegraphing something else, your audience will likely assume you're being duplicitous. An example of this is when you say something like "I'm available for questions" while your arms are crossed. When confronted with these differing messages, your audience hears one thing but sees the opposite and has to choose between the two. Since body language is an instinctive, unpremeditated language that showcases your genuine intentions, they'll often choose the nonverbal message without even consciously realizing it.

Let's go back to the examples of presidents. Remember Bill Clinton and his prolifically expressive thumb? It signaled to the audience that everything was okay. It announced to your brain that you should approve of, and feel good about, what he was saying. Barack Obama used a similar gesture throughout his residency as one of the most powerful individuals on earth. In general, his body language, posture, and hand movements were significant in his ability to elicit confidence from his supporters.

Like him or not, Donald Trump is perhaps the king of hand gestures. Take his hands up, palms out go-to posture, for instance. It sends a signal to his audience's brain that a situation is potentially dangerous. This allows him to tee up the solution he wants to convey in relation to the obstacle he simultaneously threw his hands up about. He is able to persuade a lot of people that he has the solution to many threatening situations. Whether you're convinced this polarizing figure did or did not have these answers, it's hard to deny that his hand gestures played a role in his success as a highly influential individual.

Try to be keenly aware of your body as you speak, particularly when you're rehearsing your delivery. The more you practice good body language skills, the more it will start to manifest naturally. Know, for example, that as your message changes from darker subject matter to more optimistic, you need to make sure your demeanor does as well. I like to use Shakespeare's quote from Hamlet, "Suit the action to the word, the word to the action." Your audience will be taking cues from what your expressions and body language are telling them. Make sure your physical actions aren't confusing them and potentially detracting from your message.

They Follow Him, Though He Sits

KEEPING YOUR MOVEMENT SIMPLE AND ESSENTIAL

One who does not touch the stillness within and without will invariably get lost in the movement.

—- Sadhguru

Have you heard of the Indian spiritual guru Jagadish Vasudev, better known as Sadhguru? If you haven't, do yourself a favor and look him up. He's a tremendously powerful speaker, and he has some truly profound things to offer his listeners.

He also has 8 million Instagram followers as of this publication. You read that right — close to 8 million followers! And he does all of his speaking engagements while *sitting down*. Here is living proof that being simple and grounded is enough if you have the right message and delivery. Sadhguru has the composure and confidence to hold his audience's attention for hours at a time, without ever leaving his chair.

During auditorium engagements, I'm a big proponent of holding your ground in the middle of the stage and moving only to make a point. I often get the question: "But if I stand in one spot, won't people get bored?" My answer is that it all depends on your message and delivery. If the execution of your message isn't strong, no amount of pacing is going to assuage that. If you make sure you're speaking in a genuine and powerful way, you won't need to fill gaps by wandering around the stage. Sadhguru is a perfect illustration of this.

This doesn't mean you mustn't ever move while delivering your message. If traveling to a certain spot on stage helps amplify a talking point, then go ahead and take a little cross. If the audience is spread out and it allows you to directly address more listeners, then spend some time in front of house-left and house-right. Finally, if it helps you get some nervous energy out of your system, use movement (modestly) in order to keep yourself from getting stiff or stuck.

Just make sure your audience isn't going to feel like they're watching a tennis match. The best time to move onstage is during transitions in your presentation. Once you have everything outlined, it'll be pretty clear as to when it's a good time to move and when it isn't. But, be keenly aware that people are much more likely to be distracted by too much movement than by not enough. Being grounded and owning your stillness conveys confidence and a command of what you're offering people.

PART FOUR: YOUR AUDIENCE

Ready, Aim, Fire!

DO NOT TAKE YOUR EYES OFF YOUR OBJECTIVE

The odds of hitting your target go up
dramatically when you aim at it.

— Malachi Pancoast

Now that you've read chapter 2 and know precisely what your objective is, you need to pursue it with relentless zeal. So many speakers are wonderful at developing the goal of their presentation or meeting and then abandon it once they have an audience in front of them. They end up meandering off on tangents and wasting precious time because they lose sight of why they're at their engagement in the first place. I've dedicated two chapters to this subject because it needs to be addressed in two different ways. Once when preparing, and again when presenting.

Remember: objectives motivate everything in life. They are the core driving forces behind all human behavior. This is why it's essential to keep focusing on your objective throughout your message. Take your eyes off the prize and it will show in your presentation. Conversely, the more you keep your focus on your objective as you speak, the more you'll be able to deliver your intended goals to your audience. One of the other nice benefits of staying fully focused on your objective is it will keep you from thinking about the things you want to be avoiding anyways, such as nerves. You only have a total of 100 percent capacity in your mind. If all of that is concentrated on the message you're trying to impart to your audience, there's no room for the extraneous stuff.

That's not to say your mind won't ever wander into areas it shouldn't. You're human after all. When you notice yourself waver, just steer your attention back to the intention behind your message. This will keep you on track and assure you give your listeners what you intended to offer them. If you're someone who meditates, you can use the principles of your mindfulness practice to apply it to this concept. The mind will wander, but just keep aiming it back toward your target.

Oh, You Thought This Was About You?

DON'T FORGET, IT'S *ALWAYS* ABOUT YOUR AUDIENCE

It's not about you. It's about them.

— Clint Eastwood

Here's another subject that absolutely needs to be addressed twice. Once regarding your preparation, as discussed in chapter 1, and again in respect to the delivery of your material. Your prep work amounts to nothing if you don't follow through with it. Don't do all that challenging and amazing work figuring out who your audience is and then neglect them when you're speaking. You must consciously, and unceasingly, keep steering your focus back to your listeners and what they'll be taking away from your talk.

Think back to a time when you walked away from a conversation with someone and thought, "That was one of the best verbal exchanges of ideas I've ever had!" I'll let you in on a little secret: it wasn't just you who made that conversation so wonderful. The person you were speaking to had a significant role in making you feel that way. They listened well and asked questions. They were present. And perhaps most importantly, they were equally as interested in you as they were in themselves. They took a genuine interest in who you were and what you wanted to get out of the conversation.

On the flip side, there's not much worse than being in a one-sided conversation where the person you're speaking with only talks about themself. They want you to know how intelligent they are, all the places they've visited, and the many high-profile people they've worked alongside.

The same principles apply when you're speaking to more than one person. No matter how many people are in the room with you, each individual wants to be seen and understood. They want to know that the person trying to inform them on a given subject has their best interests in mind. They're much less likely to listen to someone who is only concerned about how they appear or how much intelligence they can attempt to project to their audience.

Here's how this all ties in with the previous chapter on objectives. The more you keep your focus on the intention behind your message, the more you'll be making sure your audience comes first. That's because your goal is to increase *their* knowledge.

Think about it in terms of doctors you've visited. Don't you want them to be fully focused on *you*? When you have an ailment that you need diagnosed and healed, you want that doctor to put their singular focus on accurately treating you. You don't need to hear about what medical school they graduated from or the last person they performed surgery on. You simply want them to be present and make you feel better. The thing that will keep you coming back as a repeat patient is if they actually helped you.

So, keep reminding yourself throughout your presentation to keep it all about your audience, and the message you're trying to convey to them, and the rest will naturally fall into place.

They're Telling You Something, Are You Listening?

HOW TO VISUALLY LISTEN TO YOUR AUDIENCE

Actions do speak louder than words.
Watch what a person does more than what he says.

— Robert Kiyosaki

Because everything revolves around your audience and the message you're sending them, you absolutely must watch for the feedback your listeners are giving you. Sometimes this will be auditory, in the case of a presentation or pitch where people are actively participating. However, much of the time it will be physical cues you'll have to rely on to help guide you.

Remember the expression "The eyes are the window to the soul?" The more eyeballs you can connect with, the more information you'll be gleaning from your listeners. Don't be concerned about picking up every little nuance. As previously mentioned, much of our physical gestures and responses are unconscious. Likewise, much of our response to those cues will also be instinctive. If you're visually listening, the appropriate line of action will come naturally.

Observing your audience isn't limited to what you see in their eyes, however. We speak volumes through our physicality. So, if the entire room has their arms crossed and looks like they're ready to take a nap, it's time to pick up your energy. It doesn't mean all is doomed — simply make a few subtle adjustments and see how people respond. Your voice is capable of great nuance, so make sure to use your instrument in all the different ways that are available to you. Adjust your volume, pitch, and pace and see how your listeners respond.

But make sure not to get too caught up in one individual's physical gestures. If one of your audience members is slumping and has their arms crossed, that's not necessarily the average temperature of the entire room. That one person could just be having a bad day, and there's not a whole lot you'll be able to do to change that. If the majority of your listeners are physically alive and engaged, you can assume you're on the right track.

So, keep your focus on your listeners. Gauge their reactions, stay flexible, and adjust your delivery if necessary. It doesn't mean throwing the baby out with the bathwater if things don't go exactly as planned. But it does mean staying adaptable. And if one particular engagement doesn't get the response you were hoping for, don't fret — it's all useful intel for future endeavors. Journal your observations, learn from them, and use it all to kick ass the next time.

Ignore the Grizzly, Find the Panda

HOW FINDING A FRIENDLY FACE CAN MAKE YOUR LIFE EASIER

*It is during our darkest moments
that we must focus to see the light.*

— Aristotle

Okay, so you're moving right along in your presentation and things are going wonderfully. You couldn't have imagined a better start. That is, until you begin to notice that one person who looks like they'd rather be doing anything but listening to you. And now, of course, you can't *stop* noticing them. You become paranoid that this person is an indication of how everyone in the room feels. You try to stay focused but keep coming back to that one disgruntled individual, and it's completely throwing you.

Step one: don't panic. You're not the first person to go through an experience like this, and you won't be the last. It's often our human nature to focus on the negative things rather than the positive ones. That's because, as a species, we are survivors. We are hardwired to look for threats so we are able to defend ourselves against them. This dates back to the Paleolithic era when humankind had to fight off life-threatening animals in order to survive. Fortunately, things aren't quite so life or death today. But, relatively speaking, it doesn't make that steely person in the front row seem any less intimidating.

The best thing to do in this scenario is to put your attention on something else. More specifically, direct your awareness toward *someone* else. Scan the room for the friendliest, most attentive face and use that person as a secure anchor. When you need a boost, make eye contact with them and fill your enthusiasm tank again. The more you can keep your mind directed toward the positive, the more you'll forget about that isolated person who simply can't be bothered.

This doesn't mean you should put blinders on and single out your radiant friend for the entirety of the pitch. If you were to do that, your new comrade might feel put on the spot and will likely abandon ship. However, you can occasionally turn to them when you need a quick little boost of confidence.

Keep in mind: most people are pulling for you to succeed. That's because the opposite would result in a waste of their invaluable time. There will always be listeners who are inwardly supporting you as you speak, even if they don't explicitly show you their zeal. Remember that many people don't display how they're truly feeling in the workplace (or in general) for fear of being judged. Smiling and offering encouragement can feel like a vulnerable undertaking. Just know that people are there to learn, and it absolutely benefits them to be on your side. Lean into that, find a few allies, and keep your mind focused on the positive.

And if you're an audience member at a presentation, go ahead and pay it forward by offering the speaker some positive energy. Give them a smile, an attentive posture, or a gracious bit of feedback afterward. However you choose to show your appreciation, don't be hesitant to act on it. One of my favorite pieces of advice I've ever received was "Offer compliments freely and without reservation. It might be the most valuable thing a person hears that day, and it doesn't cost you a dime." Remember that charity doesn't always involve money. Sometimes it's just a smile or a friendly gesture offered to someone who needs it. Consequently, when the tables are turned and you're the one in the spotlight, that person you propped up will be more inclined to return the favor.

Spread the Wealth

TIPS ON ADDRESSING
A LARGE AUDIENCE

Be somebody who makes everybody feel like somebody.
— Brad Montague

For those of you speaking to a large audience, you'll most likely find it difficult to make eye contact with everyone in the room. Therefore, when addressing a big group of people, I recommend splitting your audience into three sections: left, right, and center. As you deliver your message, spend several moments in one section and then move on to the next and do the same with that group. Make sure you're not only addressing the first few rows. Scan toward the back as well. Those people are just as important and need to feel like you're equally interested in their development too. Make individual eye contact when you can; and when you can't, pick a spot within one of those sections and stay with it for a few moments, then move on to another. Essentially, you're trying to spread the wealth. This way when you're finally asked to speak to several hundred people at an industry conference, every single person in the room will feel just as important as the next.

Either You Win or You Learn

HOW TO HANDLE MISTAKES

*My biggest thrill is when I plan something and it fails. My mind
is then filled with ideas on how I can improve it.*
—- Soichiro Honda

In 1948, Soichiro Honda started a bicycle motor company in a wooden shack in Hamamatsu, Japan. That little enterprise has now grown into an international, multi-billion dollar company that produces everything from lawn equipment, to cars, to humanoid robots. It's a remarkable journey, made even more interesting when you consider the trials and tribulations the company went through.

Throughout his career, Mr. Honda encountered a multitude of setbacks. However, he always looked at those obstacles as opportunities to learn and grow. The fact that Mr. Honda viewed letdowns as a catalyst for improvement is a big reason he was able to grow his company into one of the biggest and most successful in the world.

Honda isn't the only successful entrepreneur who believed in the power of turning lemons into lemonade. Have a look at what some of the world's greatest successes have said about taking one step back but two steps forward. "Failure is another stepping stone to greatness." – Oprah Winfrey. "Sometimes when you innovate, you make mistakes. It is best to admit them quickly and get on with improving your innovations." – Steve Jobs. "It is impossible to live without failing at something, unless you live so cautiously that you might as well not have lived at all, in which case you have failed by default." – J.K. Rowling.

One of the great things about mistakes is that everyone makes them. Everyone! Even the world's most preeminent communicators, from Tony Robbins to President Barack Obama, make errors. The key is not getting too caught up in it. It's best to simply acknowledge your mistake and move along. Don't make a monumental ordeal out of it or you'll draw more attention to the blunder than is necessary. If it happens to be a large mistake that can't be dealt with in the moment, let it go and tackle it when you're able. A well thought-out email, for instance, will typically go a lot further than a knee-jerk response while you're already feeling panic-stricken.

One of the most essential things to do when these incidents come up is to accept what has happened and move forward. If you dwell on the error and beat yourself up over it, it will only serve to damage your message even more.

In those times when you do happen to make a mistake, keep in mind that it doesn't define who you are as a person. Don't jump to conclusions about your worth as a communicator, or as a human being for that matter. We all know that no one is perfect. Simply face your mistake head-on, own what happened, and then become wiser because of it.

MMA fighter Conor McGregor's coach, John Kavanagh, once said, "You're either winning or you're learning." In other words, either everything is going as you planned, or it's not and you're growing from your missteps. Simply use your setbacks as opportunities to learn and become a more powerful speaker in the future.

Do They Expect Me to Just Sit Here and Listen

HOW TO GET YOUR AUDIENCE INVOLVED

*Tell me and I forget. Teach me and
I may remember. Involve me and I learn.*

—- Benjamin Franklin

No one likes to sit through boring meetings or presentations being peppered with prosaic facts. Your mind begins to wander, you start checking your phone, or you possibly even begin to nod off to sleep. Likewise, as a speaker, it's not all that fun to merely recite a lecture by rote. Looking out to a room full of exhausted faces isn't exactly the greatest confidence booster. Involving your audience will keep them on their toes while simultaneously giving them ownership of what is being learned.

In a perfect universe, all of your listeners will be engaged, enthusiastic, and happy to participate should you want them to. However, you are the one who needs to initiate this enthusiasm and engagement. You must be willing to take the risk and encourage your listeners to actively get involved. In groups, especially unfamiliar ones, people tend to be shy and hesitant to do much else than be a passive listener. You must encourage them through your enthusiasm and leadership. Just make certain you keep the goal of the participation aimed toward offering your audience a better understanding of your message.

With your listeners in this participatory state of mind, they'll be much more likely to absorb what you say because they'll be an active part of it. Try asking a question that you allow your listeners to answer. By doing this, you'll allow for a back-and-forth and, consequently, set up an atmosphere that shows you are concerned about their thoughts and opinions. You'll also form a connection that goes beyond you solely firing information in their direction. As I've said before, this intimate connection is crucial to a great pitch, meeting, or speaking engagement.

An additional benefit of involving your audience is that it allows you to take their temperature, so to speak. I'm always encouraging my clients to listen to their audience with their eyes (see chapter 31) as well as their ears because it helps them steer the ship. When the audience has a chance to actually participate, it gives you one more tool to use in order to tweak your message on the fly. This doesn't mean you should throw your entire approach out the window. It simply means your audience will always be somewhat fluid, so you must be too.

As much as many of us would like to be the smartest person in the room, you should always be learning from your audience. Involving them will give you the opportunity to utilize the combined intellect of the entire group. Making them your ally will also take away the burden you feel to perform. It takes the pressure off your shoulders and puts the focus on your listeners.

If you decide to allow for questions and/or participation, be prepared to be asked something you don't know the answer to. In circumstances like this, it's best to let some things go. There's nothing worse than someone trying to address a subject they're not entirely familiar with. You risk the chance of being exposed as a fraud. If an inquiry comes up that you don't know the answer to, simply say, "That's a great question. Do you mind if I get back to you on that one?" They'll respect and appreciate your honesty.

Keep in mind that even if you decide you'd rather not allow audience participation, you never want to be speaking *at* your audience. It's essential to speak in a conversational yet dignified way that disarms your listeners while also drawing them in. Even though, technically, the spotlight is on you, you want the overall focus to be on them.

Swag for Everyone

GIVE THEM A TAKEAWAY

*Don't judge each day by the harvest
you reap, but by the seeds you plant.*
— Robert Louis Stevenson

Remember that you always want your listeners to leave the room (or the virtual meeting) with something mentally stimulating to contemplate. You've prepared the meeting, pitch, or presentation for a reason: to educate your counterparts with something that can improve their livelihood or their lives in general. You need them to leave smarter than when they came in. If not, then what was the point? Always keep your mind laser-focused on this goal.

I discuss the topic of objective numerous times in this book for a reason. It's crucial to the success of the message you're delivering. This goes for one-on-one conversations as much it does a larger engagement. Always approach your leadership role with the intention of offering something for your audience to walk away with. It will help motivate and give direction to your interactions and make things more efficient and effective.

One method to keep your audience thinking about your message well beyond the hour or so you're presenting is to give them an idea to ponder when they leave. This could take the form of a question or an action, or anything you think is appropriate to the subject matter. To go one step further, offer them a series of things to think about, or work on, every day of that week. This way you'll have them contemplating your message so regularly they'll likely hang onto it well beyond those initial few days. This will help reinforce your content, and fosters the endurance of that connection you worked so hard to form while they were in the room with you.

PART FIVE: YOU

Nobody Likes a Phony

LET YOUR PERSONALITY COME THROUGH

Be yourself; everyone else is already taken.

—- Oscar Wilde

You cannot expect others to accept you if you haven't learned to accept yourself first. When was the last time you heard someone say, "That person was such a phony, I really enjoyed talking to them!" Perhaps in sarcasm only. The truth is, people appreciate genuine, authentic human beings. We prefer it when folks are themselves, and we tend to absorb more of what those people say. The fact of the matter is, no matter how hard you try, you can't be someone else. They have the one and only key to that identity, just as you are the sole proprietor of yours. By all means, be inspired by people. Watch your favorite speakers and learn from them. And pay particular attention to how much of *their* personality comes through.

You have to risk being a little vulnerable to accomplish authenticity. But, I assure you, it's far more compelling to listen to an emotionally available person speak than to witness someone desperately attempting to be someone else. Be proud of who you are and the beliefs you hold. If you can offer a personal and revealing anecdote, do it. This will help get the audience on your side, and is a quick bridge to trust. And trust is half the battle. No matter how strong your message is, if your listeners don't have faith in you, they won't listen. Take ownership of who you are and allow yourself to be seen. It's so exhausting trying to be someone you're not anyway.

I recall an experience in grad school when I was participating in an exercise where the entire class gathered in a circle and stated something kind about every classmate in the room. It was a wonderfully informative assignment, and one that I occasionally use with my college students.

When it was my turn to listen to what my classmates had to say, I was taken aback by all the genuinely kind things people shared. In all honesty, it was such a long time ago that I don't remember the specifics of many of the comments. However, I certainly remember the overall feeling.

One student's remark, though, sticks with me to this day. As the last person to speak, she sat directly beside me and very sincerely offered this observation: "Cobey, I really appreciate how you want to be liked by everyone." It caught me off guard. I had just spent the last fifteen minutes listening to my classmates share these rather generous observations about me. But this particular one struck me as more of a barb than a compliment. I'm quite certain my face turned red with embarrassment as I thought, "Isn't that just a passive-aggressive way of saying I'm insecure or needy?"

As is typical of human nature, I thought about this one particular comment for the rest of the day. The remark played on a loop in my head as I kept trying to figure out the meaning of it. What were her intentions? Was she trying to insult me, or was she simply attempting to say something kind, but delivered it in an awkward way?

Regardless of her intentions, I ultimately decided what it meant to me. It actually turned out to be a gift in disguise. It highlighted the fact that I was trying far too hard to be everything to everyone.

I have always been a teacher at heart, and that often translates into being a sort of caregiver. When you choose to be an educator, you're choosing to put the needs of others before yours in order for your students to learn and grow. Sometimes that results in ignoring how you truly feel about something in deference to how you think someone else wants you to feel. This slippery slope can then turn into you hiding your true self so that everyone will like and respect you. You wind up rejecting the authentic you so that no one else can beat you to it.

I may not have liked hearing that classmate's comment on that particular day, however, I'm forever grateful for the idea she shared. It encouraged me to promise myself that I should always offer my authentic point of view, no matter what people think. Consequently, I've found that people tend to appreciate this version of me even more. They're ultimately getting the unique and singular blueprint that is Cobey Mandarino, rather than some composite of what I might think everyone wants.

Give Em A Break, Will Ya?

FIND SOME HUMOR, REGARDLESS OF THE SUBJECT

Happiness is found in not taking yourself too seriously.

-- Unknown

Humor can go a long way in winning over your audience. If you can get an audience to laugh, you're essentially getting them to increase their dopamine and serotonin levels in real time. You're giving them an endorphin rush that will almost certainly help you in your cause. You'll also be giving them an energy hit. An audience that's laughing isn't nodding off. They're more apt to be awake, alert, and ready to learn. Additionally, laughing gives your listeners a sense of relief from what might be an otherwise serious talk. The heavier the subject matter, the more you might need to inject a little humor in your delivery in order to offer your listeners a reprieve. If your topic is particularly dry or intense, it's always good to give those in the room the opportunity to take a breather from the topic. Furthermore, it will help them remember the points that are sandwiched by your lighter touches.

I Feel the Need… The Need to Not Speed

WHY YOU ABSOLUTELY MUST BE COMFORTABLE IN SILENCE AND A MEASURED PACE

Saying nothing… sometimes says the most.

— Emily Dickinson

Nothing shows nerves more than racing through your speech like you're at the Indy 500. Not to mention, when you speed through your meeting or pitch, it's hard for your listeners to keep up with you. Remember that they've never heard what you're saying before. They may understand the concepts, but this is the first time they're hearing things from your unique perspective. You must make sure to slow down so your audience can keep up.

Let's revisit that Navy SEALs quote shared earlier: "Slow is smooth, and smooth is fast." This is incredible advice coming from a group of individuals who have to perform very precise maneuvers under extremely difficult circumstances with very high stakes. Think of your presentation like a tactical maneuver. You must take your time so you aren't making critical mistakes that leave your listeners in the woods.

Some of you, no doubt, will be dying to get to the end, because you simply want to get through what feels like torture. However, you might as well not have put yourself through the torment in the first place, because your listeners will be lost if you barrel through everything. If you're going to bother speaking at all, do it with patience. Breathe, take your time, use pauses, and make your points strongly.

Silence is a wonderful way to slow things down, and is one of the most important tools you can use as a dynamic speaker. Pick spots in your talk that you absolutely need to have land on your listeners, and pause after you say them. Let things sink in. As previously mentioned, an audience really only picks up about 15 to 20 percent of what you say. The phrases that are going to stick out are the ones you emphasize and frame in silence. Those words are then able to marinate for your audience.

Think of pauses as if they were a comma, a period, or a paragraph change in writing. How challenging would reading be if authors never used these devices and merely wrote endless run-on sentences? We'd be lost much of the time as our brains attempted to separate the thoughts. The same thing happens when you don't use punctuation while you're speaking. There's nothing separating the ideas and everything begins to collide together. Consequently, your audience becomes bewildered as they play catch up while attempting to make sense of things.

A client once told me she disliked when speakers paused for effect. She possessed a remarkably strong personality which often caused her to do everything in hyperdrive. Though she was extremely intelligent, her delivery was often rushed and muddled, leaving her audiences feeling bulldozed and confused. She had been made aware of this tendency by a supervisor, which is why she had sought my help.

Working on the passion pitch exercise in one of our sessions, she had an epiphany about the importance of slowing down and using pauses. She was recounting how in her younger years she was always torn about traveling. Though she typically loved the experience once she was at her destination, she disliked how tiring and stressful the process could be.

While practicing her delivery, she spontaneously added the phrase "I have so much fear of the unknown" as an additional reason that often prevented her from traveling. She paused before and after the phrase, setting those eight words apart from the rest, as if on an island. The phrase stood out like a beacon for me to hone in on. It was as if she colored it in yellow highlighter, causing it to be separated from the rest of her delivery. In addition to the pace change, I also saw something change in her demeanor.

When she finished, she sheepishly smiled and stated, "I get it, Cobey." In that instinctive moment while she was speaking, something clicked for her. It was not only genuine and impactful for me, her audience, it was also significant and inspirational to her. Slow and steady wins the race.

Don't overuse silence, though. Sprinkle pauses in modestly. The amount of silence you can afford to use depends on the length of your engagement, of course. Gauging this correctly requires practice. At first it may feel indulgent to take a break, leaving your audience with, seemingly, nothing. You may also feel like your listeners will become impatient for the next bit of information. But rest assured, your listeners will not only be okay with those moments, they will welcome them with open arms. Their minds will have the opportunity to take a break, which will also keep them fresh and on their toes. Become comfortable with silence and you will, undoubtedly, become a better communicator.

Because the Hook Brings You Back

WHY YOU SOMETIMES JUST
NEED TO SAY IT AGAIN

There is no harm in repeating a good thing.

—- Plato

Back in my days as a performer, I quickly learned the vital importance of making the name or tagline of a product stand out while working on commercials, corporate videos, and voiceovers. There is a particular way to say "Microsoft" so that it is illuminated and the listener hooks onto it. From my extensive work with this company, I also became aware of how often repetition was used in copywriting to allow things to stand out. Their writers understand just how to reiterate their message so that it reverberates in the listeners' ears without them even consciously being aware of it. That's part of the trick. Sometimes you want to persuasively tap your listeners on the shoulder, rather than hit them over the head with an anvil.

Once you've got a solid grip on your message, find different ways to repeat it. Flip it on its head, repurpose it, finesse it.

Make sure your audience knows exactly what they came for without boring them to death with the same words over and over. Keep them on their toes.

That's not to say you shouldn't ever repeat things word-for-word. It's important to keep in mind that a live audience doesn't have the luxury of a rewind button. They may miss some things, because people zone out sometimes. Audience members also make noises at inopportune times. So, it's crucial that if you have something to say that folks absolutely cannot leave without hearing, make sure you repeat it. Back-to-back and word-for-word, if necessary. Think of your message like the chorus of a song. You want your listeners to have that refrain stuck in their head for the rest of the day, or even the week.

Uhh This Chapter Is Like Ya-Know About Useless Umm Fillers

SHOW YOUR CONFIDENCE BY AVOIDING FILLERS

The most valuable of all talents is that of
never using two words when one will do.

—- Thomas Jefferson

An exercise I often work on with many of my clients is the "um" and "uh" test. I have them share their passion pitch with me, and each time they serve up a filler word, I stop them and have them start over from the beginning.

One of the biggest distractions for an audience member is a speaker who is constantly interrupting themselves with these unnecessary filler words. Uhh, imagine if I, uhh, did this while I, umm, wrote. This book would be tedious to read, as well as many pages longer than necessary.

This extraneous verbal padding is often uttered out of habit. It serves as a crutch to take you from one thought to another. Shorten the distance to your objective by taking out those needless bridges. Start paying attention when you're speaking to *anyone* how often you add sounds that don't need to be in the conversation. It doesn't matter if it's in a meeting or at the grocery store. The more you notice them, the more they'll start to bother you. You'll then begin to naturally remove them from your habitual speech patterns.

The American digital artist Mike Winkelmann, better known as Beeple, was a guest on the Joe Rogan Experience podcast in December 2021. Though entertaining, he used the filler word "like" in his conversation so often that Rogan finally pointed out how distracting he found it. After dropping several hints, Rogan finally blurted out, "Do you hear all the 'likes' coming out of your mouth?"

Rogan's remark was refreshing, as well as validating. While listening to the podcast, I kept thinking, "I wonder if anyone else is as distracted by this as I am." Granted, it's my job to hear those verbal habits and behaviors. But like me, Rogan was clearly thinking the podcast would be more palatable if Winkelmann stopped interjecting "like" into every sentence. And if we both picked up on it, chances are pretty good that a fair portion of Rogan's 11 million listeners noticed it as well. Even if it was only 10 percent of his fan base, that's over a million people getting frustrated with Winkelmann and his use of the word "like."

If you've been using these extraneous words your entire life, they aren't that easy to eradicate. Rogan couldn't expect Winkelmann to suddenly stop doing something he had most likely been unconsciously doing for years. That's why it's essential to start noticing those filler words now so you can eventually eliminate them. Hire a communication coach and insist it's one of the first things you work on. Hey, Beeple, if you're reading this, give me a call. I can, like, help you out.

Even Einstein Was Controversial

NEVER APOLOGIZE FOR WHAT YOU HAVE TO OFFER

Even when it's not popular, we must hold onto the truth.

— Keith Green

A big error that anxious speakers make is apologizing for or qualifying their ideas. When we are feeling nervous or insecure, we might say things such as "This is just my opinion…" or "You might have a different philosophy…." This puts you on the back foot and weakens your message. First, be sure to thoroughly research all of your facts so you feel confident about the information you are discussing. Second, once you are assured of your content, practice your talk in front of colleagues or friends. Every time a caveat or qualifier is added, have your friends signal that you need to start over. The strongest communicators realize that not everyone is going to agree with them. In fact, some of the best speakers are controversial on purpose. They want to shake things up and get people our of their comfort zone. Adding your unique and provocative perspective can get people thinking and keep them on their toes.

Ordinary Doesn't Move the Needle

WHY YOU SHOULDN'T BE
AFRAID TO TAKE RISKS

If you want to reach everyone in the audience,
it's not about being bigger, it's about going deeper.

-– Sanford Meisner

During one of my favorite exercises, "the passion pitch," one of my college students recounted a story about walking home from the library one night and being followed by a group of male students. She explained that they had tailed her very closely for a long period of time and were making unsavory comments in the process. She stated that even though, in hindsight, she assumed they were mostly trying to make jokes at her expense, she was terrified in the moment. While she walked alone in front of them, she had no way of knowing what their actual intentions were. The overall message of her pitch: more men should realize how vulnerable a woman can feel while walking alone at night.

When she initially delivered her pitch, she was merely retelling a story. There was no passion behind it. I could tell that deep down she felt strongly about her message, but she was holding back. I explained to her that her message was important for people to hear, but they wouldn't necessarily be affected by it unless she took a risk and spoke from the heart. If she was going to share this personal experience with strangers, holding back does her, her audience, and her message a disservice. Recounting a challenging personal experience while having little impact on your audience only causes you to have to recount something distressing with no restitution. She agreed.

I asked her to try it again, but this time suggested she first take a moment to allow herself to sense some of the fear she experienced that night. I made certain she was in a good headspace for this and was also willing to do so. I never want a student to further traumatize themselves if they feel a wound is still too deep or fresh. She responded by saying that the only reason she was holding back was because she didn't want her audience to feel uncomfortable. I assured her that, in this particular case, you *need* your audience to feel a little uneasy. That sensation is exactly what is going to cause people to change.

She closed her eyes and took a deep breath. A few moments passed before her eyes fluttered back open and she began to speak. This time I could see the expression in her eyes. She remained composed but her words came from the heart. It was powerful. And though her eyes remained dry while she spoke, the rest of the class was in tears. They were moved because *she* was moving them by way of her deep personalization.

He Went Out for Milk but Got a Burger

THE POWER OF CONNECTION

Connection is why we're here; it is what
gives purpose and meaning to our lives.

—- Brené Brown

How important is connection to you when communicating? When you go into your doctor's office to tell them you've been dealing with a mysterious health issue, how connected would you like them to be as they give you their prognosis? How about when you're chatting with your financial advisor about an important investment decision? Do you want them to be completely present and engaged with you, or would you rather they just give you their advice by rote?

We often take for granted the importance of connection when we're pitching to investors, presenting at a public speaking engagement, or simply in a company meeting. If we're good at what we do, we'll rely on our intelligence and the degree of our preparation. But far too often when we pass our knowledge and know-how on to others, we miss one of the most important parts of communication. We neglect the significance of connection.

In preparing for an engagement, you may have conducted heaps of research and put together a splashy PowerPoint that would make your mom proud. However, if you're not genuinely connecting, you're going to lose a lot of listeners in the process. No one says you have to win over every single person in the room. In fact, depending on the size of the crowd, there's a decent chance you might not. There is only so much you can do for the person who's been ready to leave the room ever since they entered. However, if there's at least one individual in your audience who is ready to connect, it's to your advantage to build that bridge for them. They came to learn, they're emotionally present, they want to connect. Therefore you must be ready to be of service in that way.

Connection is more than just speaking the words and having others hear and understand them. It goes to a deeper level. When you connect, you inspire people. You motivate them to buy-in to what you're pitching. It's the difference between being acknowledged for doing a "good job" and getting top-notch investors excited to be a part of your project.

So how do you connect? Oftentimes it's as simple as merely setting that intention before you begin. It's something we often take for granted, but we set intentions for just about everything we do. Think of this analogy: how does the milk that you buy get into your refrigerator? You go to the grocery store, take the milk off the shelf, pay for it, and then drive it home. But what made you go to the store in the first place? You set the intention. You said to yourself, "I need milk," and so you went and did it. And though you may not be consciously aware of it, you kept that intention throughout your task. It's why you picked up the milk instead of, say, detouring to grab a burger at In-N-Out.

But dairy acquisition is a no-brainer — you don't usually have to keep reminding yourself to pick up the 2% while you're on your trip to the grocery store. However, when you're presenting a business idea to colleagues or potential clients, it's obviously a little more challenging. There are countless stress factors involved that may distract you from remembering to stay connected. Did I do enough research? Are people listening? Do I have something on my face? Therefore, you have to consistently remind yourself to stay present and connect.

It takes practice. Think about the milk analogy. Staying on task comes easily because you've done it so many times. However, connecting may be something that isn't in your usual repertoire. Therefore, you need to practice it every day. Train yourself with as many people you encounter throughout the week. Practice it with your kids. Children have an amazing ability to live in the present moment. Though it may be fleeting, they're constantly connecting because they don't have a lot of life history to bog them down, while also not having many responsibilities that keep their mind reaching towards the future. Practice with them and notice how well you can connect from moment to moment.

No children? Rehearse with your therapist. I believe that a therapist is not hired simply to listen to your problems. Hopefully you've retained their services to also allow you to practice being your best self. Get the most out of that $200/hour session. Utilize them to get plugged in.

No children, no therapist? No problem. Try it out with friends, or even that Trader Joe's employee. You don't even have to tell them it's happening. Just be present and make an effort to connect. If you practice connecting on a daily basis, it'll be that much easier when you're presenting in front of a group of intimidating people who are calculating return-on-investment possibilities with every sentence you utter.

Need more reason to connect? It's been scientifically proven that connecting with others lowers the tendency toward depression while simultaneously heightening self-esteem.[8] Connection is a primal, fundamental human need. There's a reason we have lived and traveled in tribes since the dawn

---

[8] Seppala, Emma, PhD. 2014. Connectedness and Health: The Science of Social Connection. Stanford Medicine.

of humankind. So, set your intention, put yourself out there, and connect.

Mamma Mia, I'm the Dancing Queen

REMEMBER TO ALWAYS
HAVE A LITTLE FUN

*Having fun is not a diversion from a
successful life; it is the pathway to it.*

—- Martha Beck

When I began my acting career, I generally dismissed the idea of having any fun. I idolized brooding performers like Montgomery Clift and Steve McQueen and felt I was only doing my job if I was off in a corner in between scenes torturing myself in order to get into character. It made no difference whether I was acting in *Hamlet* or a commercial for Subaru. I wanted to effect change, and didn't think I could do that if I was actually enjoying things. I saw myself as a serious artist who related more to Marlon Brando than Neil Patrick Harris. No disrespect to Mr. Harris, it's just I had no intentions of ever performing in a musical. I could barely muster the desire to work on commercials because my idealistic mindset saw that as selling out.

Anyone who has ever been in the business will tell you an approach like that is a fast pass to not working very often. First of all, not many people want to work with someone who doesn't ever leave character (Daniel Day-Lewis notwithstanding). And handpicking your projects so you only work on "serious" material is a quick way to unemployment. If you're smart, you soon realize you need to say "yes" to just about everything in order to make a living at your craft.

Like anyone else, I would occasionally lose sight of the positive spirit that kept me working for so many years. My intense artist side would come out and I would need a reminder that a career should involve a good amount of levity and joy. No matter what you do.

I had just come off a project that had been very dark, inhabiting a character that was deeply personal. Roles like these would often make me view my craft with an earnestness and ego that was not always the healthiest. Particularly if accolades were involved. But, as mentioned before, I was fortunate enough to have reminders that kept things in check.

Case in point, my next production found me performing in one of the most whimsical musicals to have ever hit the stage. I was cast as Harry in the ABBA jukebox musical, *Mamma Mia*. When I accepted the gig, still in the vapor trails of my previous production, it was primarily because of the impressive paycheck. I wasn't terribly excited about the material. I figured I would just show up to the theatre, do the work, and keep my fingers crossed I wouldn't get bored along the way.

Little did I realize how much fun I would actually have. The cast was terrific to work with, the character was a blast to explore, and it was an overall joy to be a part of that production. Perhaps the main reason this show was such an outstanding experience, though, was because of our audiences. They came to have fun. And they did just that, night after night. Had I not stumbled upon this realization and failed to have fun with them, I most likely would have ruined it for everyone (including myself).

Every evening as I arrived at the theatre I would be greeted by joyous people in lines stretching around the block. They were dressed in feather boas, gleefully dancing on the sidewalk, and singing "Dancing Queen" before they were even allowed inside. It dawned on me the first time I witnessed it: these people aren't here to experience theatre the way I had thought it should be experienced when I started my career. They didn't want to leave the production pondering their ideals and the meaning of life. They simply wanted to have some silly, sing-out-loud, dance-in-the-aisles fun. They wanted to celebrate.

COBEY MANDARINO

Night after night we would perform for a sold-out audience of 2,000 people. And at every performance, without fail, those 2,000 theatre-goers would jump out of their seats and roar in excitement when we would perform the finale. If you're not familiar with the show, the ending is essentially a mini-concert that crams in the remaining ABBA songs that the writers couldn't fit into the story. I'll admit, I felt a little like a rock star — I think we all did. I will never forget the euphoric feeling it gave me, show after show.

What if I had kept the blinders on and never adapted to our audience? What if I kept stubbornly performing as if I were playing *Hamlet* at The Globe Theatre in London? I would have come off as highly pretentious and probably looked pretty ridiculous in the process. I would've ruined it for all those audience members. They came to have fun and I would have sedated them instead.

Take a look at all the great speakers you come across and you'll find that the powerful ones share a trait. They're all enjoying themselves. It may manifest in different ways depending on the subject matter, but deep inside there's a passion and a joy for what they're doing. Your approach to communicating should be no different. Your audience, no matter who they are, will always choose to enjoy human interactions over not. They want to relish their jobs and enjoy as much of their lives as possible. And when you're with them, their enjoyment rests on your willingness to offer that when speaking to them.

By all means, take your work seriously. Do your research, show up on time, and put your heart into what you're doing. But don't ever lose sight of the fact that your job is one-third of a life that is meant to be filled with happiness.

CONCLUSION

The ability to communicate effectively and confidently is one of the most important life skills to learn. You only need to observe a baby listening intently to its mother while trying to repeat the sounds that she makes to comprehend how fundamental the primal urge is to communicate. It is what enables us to pass information to other people, and to understand what is said to us.

When communication is efficient and powerful, it leaves all parties involved feeling satisfied. By delivering messages clearly, you prevent misunderstanding and/or wasted time. This ultimately increases the potential for greater productivity and better relationships, while decreasing the potential for conflict. In incidents where conflict does develop, effective communication serves as the key to ensuring that situations are resolved in an efficient and respectful manner. How we communicate is critical in allowing us to excel at a job, maintain healthy relationships, and express ourselves genuinely.

To be a confident and powerful communicator requires technique, drive, and the ability to share your vision with clarity and passion. These are the building blocks that make up the foundation of a *Fearless Captivating Unstoppable* communicator. And while some people are born with the gift of great presence and exceptional communication, anyone can develop it through skillful training and a little bit of dedication.

145

Thank you…

Glenn Davis
Scott Ellis
Laurie Gibson
Megan Gisle
Colin Hanset
Temple Northup
Tara Powell
Jeffrey Salmon
Michael Vamosy
Ira Vouk